PERCEPTIONS
ISBN 0-9645633-0-4

Cover Illustration by Danny Elliott
First printing October 1995

Thank you for your support Sharon J. Smith, and hope you enjoyed the play. You are The "Lady"
David Spencer

TABLE OF CONTENTS

THANKS

ACKNOWLEDGEMENT

Without the participation of many, the formation of my ideas behind *Perceptions* would not have been possible. My appreciation extends to all who were kind enough to take the time to share their thoughts and experiences.

My gratitude also goes to my wife Millie, for being understanding, patient, and most of all, loving during this long period. Additional thanks must be given to Juanita Fletcher, Carolyn Richards, and Gwendolyn Mitchell for their assistance during the book's infant stages. Thanks also must go to the book's project editors, Jacqueline C. Young and Christopher Greene. Thank you Helen Higginbottom for your reading evaluation and expert advice.

Finally, a definite thanks must go to Dr. Cynthia White, a consulting psychiatrist, for helping me complete part one of *Perceptions*.

WARNING

PERCEPTIONS is a fun and insightful book based on various personal experiences of women who were interviewed about their interactions with people from their past to present. Many of these responses seem to corroborate my own observations and years of everyday experience.

PERCEPTIONS, however, is not a book intended to amend any past studies on female sexuality. Originally compiled for personal record and private enlightenment, many of my friends felt **PERCEPTIONS** was something that should be shared with readers. A word of caution though: **PERCEPTIONS** is not a book you would lend to a friend, for it may never be returned. And last but not least, it is not just a book labeled "for women only." This book contains interesting observations and testimonies that can further all of our understanding of certain types of women.

Even though my first documented thoughts were written March 19, 1977, this curiosity began as far back as 1960. At the age of 16, I found the observations of people to be a great pastime passion. Even many years later, I find observing and studying people is still a great avocation. Out of these investigations, (as I call them) I discovered certain distinct types of behavior. Therefore, I feel that my observations coupled with testimonies and personal experiences serve a similar purpose as other clinical or lab-tested findings. My deductions resulted in a method that helped me to identify how to approach women who seemed to fit in one or more categories. Although labeling is done by everyone, most people don't like to be labeled, generalized, or categorized in any shape or form by others.

The truth of the matter is, we all, at least subconsciously, label the people we meet. As we grow older, we take on likenesses and patterns of others around us. Most of us have examined the characteristics of our astrological signs. This in itself further categorize us. Besides that, all of us have our own method of assessing other peoples' personality and thus place a label on them as being a certain type of person. I have organized my findings by categorizing people according to similar traits. The results have been interesting. On the other hand, I make suggestions one can develop into his or her own personality and lifestyle.

Part one of PERCEPTIONS is meant to provide the reading audience with a taste of things to come. What I have accomplished with the first eight chapters is to give the public a fun, informative way to look at women from various points of views. I want to reiterate that PERCEPTIONS is not a book meant to replace any previous research on male-female relationships. It is not the Hite Report or a Masters and Johnson research. It is a fun book that is based on many years of interviews with women about how they perceive the world around them and how they think the world perceives them.

When I started out, I was looking for answers in developing better communications between me and my friend. I was the talkative one whereas my friend was the quiet one. That was unusual because it was just the opposite when I was around other people. They were the ones that wanted to talk to me and I was the willing listener. I was always interested in knowing what people thought about or wondered why they did some of the things they did. My initial intent was to obtain a better understanding of my friend and to stimulate better communication between us. In the beginning, I would ask women I knew what I needed to do or say to enhance the comfort level of my friend. I would describe my situation and ask them for their advice. It wouldn't be long into our conversation before they would begin disclosing things about their private lives. Although I was flattered they felt that comfortable enough to open up to me as they did, I wasn't getting any direct help on my request. After a while, I decided to randomly ask women I did not know.

My primary question was always the same, "Do you think both mates should be able to talk about anything, especially about sex?" The answers were always the same from everyone who I had asked this question of. "Yes!" Most women said they wish they could talk to their mates about anything without him getting upset. That was when they started talking about their own relationships. I found it very interesting how so many women did not mind me asking very personal questions. Some gave me more details than others. The fact is, everyone I talked with told me something about themselves that they would not or have not told to either their mates or best friends. All of this was helping me to understand women more, but it wasn't getting me any closer to stimulating a dialogue between me and my friend. I would discuss with her some conversations I had, with the hope that this would open her up. It never did. That did not stop me from asking more women about their ideas on open communication with their mates. I gradually developed questions that I had asked and wanted to ask my friend. My friend had always felt I was getting too personal with her. So after a while, I stopped asking her.

In the meantime though, I was developing a very strong interest in wanting to know more from other women. I wanted to find out how many women felt certain kinds of things. That was when I began structuring my written questionnaire. At that same time, I purchased a pocket-sized notepad to record my documented responses from the interviewees. It wasn't difficult to get women from all walks of life to participate in my interview process. I would explain to them that I was gathering data

At first, some women felt a man could not write a book about women. But I assured them it was not going to be a book on how I perceive women, but how women perceive men and other women. After about a year, I started noticing that certain questions were getting answered with similar responses. Then there were other questions that most women had answered in the same fashion. That is how I derived the Universal Concept for All Free-Thinking Women.

PERCEPTIONS has gone through several name changes over the years. The first name selected was "The Book." Then I changed it to "Characters." Next I changed it to "Table of Contents," and finally, to PERCEPTIONS. It became clear to me that I was collecting perceptions from women about themselves, other people, and how they would like to be perceived.

Part one of PERCEPTIONS has identified ten fun personality types. PERCEPTIONS II will identify six more fun types. These selected types are not conclusive of all the types of women in the world. Each woman is unique and has her own distinct personality. However, we all have similar traits of another person. PERCEPTIONS is a collection of these traits as related by the many interviews that were conducted over 17 years.

Last but most important, it is not a how-to book. Again, it is a fun book that can provide some insight about women who seem to possess certain similar personality characteristics.

THE AMAZON TYPE

THE AMAZON TYPE

Tallness has its unique and desirous advantages. Many of us have dreamed of being the tall, perfect-figured person we see repeatedly in magazines and on television. And yet, being tall also has some disadvantages.

A woman is considered tall if she is over 5 feet 7 inches, but being tall does not alone qualify her for being considered an Amazon. The Amazon is based on not only the woman's height, but also on her personality traits. However, the taller the woman is, the closer she is to being an Amazon. I have met a woman who is 6 feet tall, but she is very quiet, a shy Amazon type, which is unusual.

The term "Amazon" conjures up many different images, dating back to when we were young and watching films and movies at the neighborhood cinema. Amazon was used to refer to women found in Greek mythology who were members of a nation of female warriors reputed to have lived in Scythia, near the Black Sea and Iran. They were a group of tall, vigorous, strong-willed women, who were not dependent on men for their well-being or even for their daily existence and happiness. No men lived in their tribal communities. Yet instinctively they knew how to coexist with men, although in a more controlling manner than we know of today. They did know the special place that men held in their lives and still maintained their independence. The Amazon I describe later possesses many of these characteristics.

One of the unique attributes about an Amazon woman is that she maintains the proper weight in proportion to her bone structure. She is not a skinny woman and, actually, she is not a fat one either. It is a common trait that she is very attractive. The Amazon is often perceived as a tall, masculine woman. Unlike the fictional comic book character, *Wonder Woman,* the real Amazon type is not a member of a race of female warriors defending the world from injustice and protecting the downtrodden. Quite the contrary. She is a woman who is very strong-willed and independent. Her tallness, anchored by long legs, isn't the only noticeable trait that makes her stand out in the crowd. All of her physical features - facial, bust line, small waist, and full hips - complement her full body structure. With a height ranging from 5' 7" to 6" 0", she is hard to overlook. Again, some may perceive her as a woman defined by her big size and masculine-like features. There are many women who fit that description and may think they are Amazonian by nature. But for the purpose of this book, this is not the main characteristic of a woman who qualifies here as an Amazon. In fact, it may be more accurate to identify this type of woman as the Full Woman rather than the Amazon woman. We will discuss the Full Woman type later in this chapter, and you will see that size is only a small part of what makes her so.

The Amazon woman knows that her height causes people to stop and stare. Often, they can be overheard whispering, "Did you see that woman? Boy, is she tall. That is too tall for a woman."

Men whose heights range from 5' 6" to 5' 9" feet are instantly attracted to this type of tall, attractive woman. They know that the Amazon woman stands out and helps them to stand out even more. How can you miss seeing the pair? Especially if they are of equal height.

Although the Amazon prefers someone much taller than she is (it's good to be able to look up to someone even if you are tall), she values the height and worth of a man's ambitions and moral character more than anything else. You have to stand tall in many ways to meet this woman's needs. Let's be realistic though. A man of 5 feet 8 inches tall would be the minimum standard that a 6-feet-tall Amazon woman would consider dating for an extended period. She wants to be able to look up to her man. As a man, if you are shorter, you must have a great deal going for you to sustain the relationship. Being with a tall Amazon woman can bring out the Napoleonic complex in the most socially, professionally, and personally secure man. There aren't many women who do not prefer tall men. And equally true, on the flip side, there aren't many men who prefer to have an Amazon type woman, very tall. Don't get me wrong. This is not because these men do not genuinely admire or desire these type women. The reason can be attributed more to the man's ego, haughtiness, pride, or self-esteem, which stems from his being or feeling less secure around a woman who may be (or appears to be) equal to his height, assertiveness, and strong-willed nature. It may be old-fashioned or chauvinistic, but many men still believe they should have or feel that they have physical dominance over their mates. This feeling of male dominance often creates a false sense of mental and emotional security. The Amazon woman prefers both strengths. It is important to her that a man's body composition and strength are in equal proportion to the structure of his physical frame. Above all else, his moral character has to be even stronger than his strength. You may wonder why this is so. The answer is simple. The Amazon demands so much of herself, she expects the same of her mate.

This can create problems for many men. For example, most men with shallow egos will try to overcompensate for whatever they are lacking in character by trying to exercise power and strength through their physical prowess. But without a matching personality, this type of man would not last very long with the Amazon woman. She demands a great deal of herself and her mate, and sees no need to lower her standards. She wants to be above the rest in all aspects of her life.

Most Amazon women have certain styles and characteristics about them that not only makes them tower over other women, but can, and often do, cast a shadow of mysticism as well. That mysticism stems from the legend of the Amazon woman. The legend started in the 1950's and 1960's with the Hercules and Greek film series. However, it intensified in popularity with the arrival of the "Wonder Woman" movies and television series that were successful in the late 1970's. Little girls everywhere wanted to be

Wonder Woman. They draped their necks with towels or sheets and created their own makeshift costumes if they could not talk their parents into buying the real thing. Sales of Wonder Woman paraphernalia skyrocketed. Marketing executives were hard-pressed to keep pace with the buying public's demand. Wonder Woman became a phenomenon although we knew she wasn't real.

The Amazon woman is a phenomenon, too. She appears to glide across space when she walks. As you watch her, you might notice that each step is pronounced and definitive. Her walk makes a profound statement about the direction she is going and that she definitely will get there, her way. She is a woman who is always moving forward. If she appears at times to pause or to take a backward step, watch out because she is only regrouping, preparing to take a bigger step.

Amazon women are usually very private people. They can create and live in a world that exists secretly in the middle of a very public life. It is this very public environment that makes them want to hide their vulnerabilities from the unsuspecting world.

The Amazon's childhood was probably not fun like most other little girls. Her physical attributes were probably well developed at a much earlier age than that of her peers. She was probably the first of her age group to experience many things. Always taller, bigger, stronger, and sometimes an outcast, she felt different, which when you are young is difficult anyway.

In some cases, she is a woman who was sexually abused by a family member because she always appeared to be much older than she was. If not abused, she was approached sexually by older boys or men well before her teenage years. She had to grow up much faster than her peers, often feeling out of place or a misfit. Boys her own age were not mentally or physically mature, whereas other girls had little in common with her. She had to spend too much time caught awkwardly between the world of a child and adult. Although that border may seem ideal to the average person, to the Amazon child it is a very limited, confusing, and restricted world that has not been explained to her. She has not been trained, equipped, or prepared for this woman-child world. It is from this ambiguous, paradoxical puzzle that she has had to adjust and mature fast.

In spite of it all, Amazon women are easy people to get along with. Like the Prima Donna, they just want people to accept them for who they are. An offshoot of the Amazon type is the Full Woman type. She has some traits of the Amazon, for example, height. But the Full Woman has much more body, usually because of an accompanying weight problem. These women can be considered full-figured, ranging from very large to extremely huge. Many of them have attractive faces and very pleasing personalities. Most of them have strong wills, but large appetites for food. They use food as a crutch to compensate for other things that are lacking in their lives.

The Full Woman likes to dominate her mate. You will often find her with a man much smaller and shorter than herself. Men don't always seem to object to her domineering style. They know she will take very good care of them. She knows that there are not that many available men for her, so she is willing to go the extra mile to keep her man satisfied.

The Full Woman can be as tall as the Amazon but she can also be as short as 4' 11" and still be considered the Full Woman. The Full Woman can have dominant traits that might be associated with any one of the other types of women described here in this book. Therefore, there is no special category called the Full-Woman type. It is merely a descriptive term to identify certain women who are referred to as "big women," and I felt she best fit under the Amazon category. As the world becomes more tolerant and women become more self-assured about their worth despite their size and looks, we will hear more about the Full Woman. Clothing retailers have already begun to realize that there is a market of full women just waiting to be tapped. Who knows? It may be the Full Woman who eventually controls the market, rather than vice versa.

For this chapter, I interviewed three women who had a special something about them that was particularly interesting and deserved to be mentioned separately. Their names were selected based on one of their strong points. All three had several things in common, but each had some unique attributes that compelled me to include each of them.

The first Amazon I call Ms. Shy One. As you probably have guessed, she is very shy. In fact she is extremely shy. She is 6 feet tall and relishes her height. It wasn't until near the end of our interviews that she opened up to let me see her real self that she keeps hidden inside. The one thing that stands out the most with her is discovering her erogenous area, her hot spot. A man would have to really get to know her extremely well to ever find it. This one area, she says, turns her on, regardless of any mood she may be in.

Born under the sign of Cancer, she admits that she is true to her zodiac sign and can be very moody at times. Her mood shifts swing from "quiet, grumpy, crazy, or sexy to just nice," as she put it. She likes things to be a certain way and wants people to "do the right thing." Ms. Shy One appears to be straight-laced and dull. Although she is a very sexual person, she doesn't often experience a real need for sex. But if a man knows where her "hot spot" is, he could change her mind very quickly. However, that requires that he get to know her well enough to learn where it is. In fact, if she doesn't tell him, it is improbable that he would find out, unless by sheer luck.

When she told me it was the third finger of her left hand, I tried not to let my face show how surprised I was. Without thinking, I asked her, "From which end of . . . this finger?" She smiled and coyly said, "It doesn't matter. It's still the same finger from both ends." Of course I immediately had to check this out for myself. I raised my left hand up to my face and noticed that it was the middle finger. I was somewhat embarrassed that I could not figure that one out without her having told me. Usually when a woman says third finger, left hand, I think of the wedding ring finger. Anyway, she told me that she is very protective of that finger. No man can get hold of it without her permission.

Although her shyness may have suggested that she's not assertive or strong-willed, this is not so. Her shyness was a way to preserve and protect her privacy. She stands on guard to defend her territory if there is a threat of someone getting too close. Or if someone comes too close to crossing the borderline she has established for others. It's just part of her personality.

Now, I want to discuss my second interviewee, Ms. Open-for-Business. She is a Virgo. She was something else, and I mean something else. She was the complete opposite of Ms. Shy One. We have often heard it said that they grow them big in Texas. If that is true, she was a perfect example. Her 6 feet 2 inch body was well proportioned to her bone structure. Her stride was long and steady, like that of a giraffe. She looked good in her form-fitting jeans, and the rest of her wasn't difficult to notice either. You had to be blind to not notice how good she looked. Maybe you get my point, but let me explain anyway. She told me she had a

48-D bust, with a 24-inch waist and 34-inch hips. I thought to myself, "That *is* kind of large." Whatever it was, her bust complemented the rest of her. It all fit nicely.

At 162 pounds, Ms. Open-for-Business was very attractive. Her Texan accent added that extra spice. Picture a very tall Amazon with a heavy twang in her voice. It was somewhat sexy. I was shocked when she told me she was a "call girl." I thought I had misunderstood her at first and asked her to repeat what she had said.

"I am a call girl and my fee is $100 per hour," she said.

"Didn't you tell me you are married?" I asked. There was no hesitation in her answer. Ms. Open-for-Business was very open about her business and her relationships with her three husbands. The first two husbands had been alcoholics who had physically abused her. It wasn't until after her second marriage that she turned to the world's oldest profession to earn enough money to take care of herself and her two children.

It had started with generous men who were more than willing to buy her things and give her money for the pleasure of being seen with her and being able to "show off to the fellows." At first, it was difficult for her. She did not like what she was doing. It repulsed her, but eventually she knew, or felt, that she had to remain in the "business" for her family's survival.

When she became more comfortable with our discussions, she reminisced to when she was only six years old. That was when her father started to sexually abuse her. The abuse continued until she was about 14 years old. Again, this caught me off guard and I paused before asking her anything else. When I got up the courage, I began asking questions in a nervous, shaky voice. Clearly, I was jarred by this revelation.

"What does a person *do* with a child that is only six years old?" I asked cautiously, not really certain if I were prepared for the answer that *might* be coming. She paused before she could bring herself to respond.

"I'll put it to you this way," she said. "He would put it inside me while it was soft and listen to my bones crack [sick] as he got it hard." Of course, I cringed at the thought of that and the kind of man who was sick enough to do that to his own daughter. I asked if that trauma was still haunting her now that she was a 26-year-old woman. Ms. Open-for-Business said that now she only has flashbacks, especially when she talks with other women about their lives growing up with their families. Hers was so different that she had to think about how her life was and how things could have been different if she had grown up in different circumstances. By this time, I was almost afraid to ask further questions. I was fearful of other wounds that could open or how I would react to possible answers. Fortunately, she was willing to go on, even anxious to do so, and made certain I asked her every question on the questionnaire. I had purposely skipped a couple of questions as I entered uncharted territory. Because I had the questionnaire laid out flat in easy view as I wrote my notes on it, she had noticed my skipping over certain questions and insisted I go back to those questions. I could not ignore her assertiveness.

She was very open with me all right, but I wasn't certain at times if she was "giving me the business" or not. After all, she had told me before that she was full of surprises. At this point, I did not need any more convincing, so I asked her to tell me more about her profession, which proved to be very enlightening.

She told me she gets her "clients" by telling them that she works for an escort service whenever they asked what she did for a living.

Her clients are charged according to their professional status and how quietly they want their professional arrangement kept. Most of her "clients" are from out of town, and 75% of them only want to talk, to take her out to dinner, or want to have friendly company for an evening.

Her first experience as a call girl occurred when she was only 21. Her first client approached her with a $1,000 proposition. To put it in her own words, "He came to me and offered me $1,000 for a blow-job. Well, I had an alcoholic husband who was a mama's boy and bills to pay." I really didn't need to ask if she took the man up on his offer. I knew she had. Since then, her strangest requests have been from someone who wanted to give her a jelly bath and another to become a six-foot banana split. I didn't bother asking if she accepted either proposition. I decided I would just wonder about it.

Ms. Open-for-Business was an interesting person to listen to and have one of those heart-to-heart conversations with. She mentioned that men found her fascinating, not necessarily because of her size or measurements but because she was full of surprises. She also pointed out that she was "damn good" at her profession, and never had a complaint! I couldn't let the interview end without asking the obvious. The last thing I wanted to know about was her husband.

"Does he know about your business?" I asked.

"Yes," she said, as if to say "Of course."

"How does he handle it?"

"He is not insecure about the relationship at all."

According to Ms. Open-for-Business, her husband is the perfect physical man for her. "My husband is 5 feet 8 inches , with dark hair, fair eyes, average-looking, not too heavy, not too skinny, and one hell of a lover."

Anyway you look at it, his ego must be very strong, especially if he accepts the profession she is in. A hell of a lover? I think he must be one hell of a man, period.

The third woman I'll call is Ms. Wonder Woman. This is the Amazon type of woman we associate more with the stereotyped legend. She is the tall, beautiful, courageous, aggressive, assertive, and strong-willed woman. My Amazon model fits this description.

Ms. Wonder Woman is 5 feet 11 inches and is a Virgo. The zodiac signs play an important role in distinguishing the uniqueness of each of us. But actually, our lives are shaped more by our experiences, all of which are perceived by our five plus one senses. We are what we think we are and what we allow others to convince us that we are. Yes, there are forces that influence the way we think and how we view ourselves. Height is the common trait that shapes how Ms. Wonder Woman thinks. She is a successful business woman who I have admired from a distance for several years. I have seen her emerge as a professional woman working for others to owning her own business and becoming her own boss. I have witnessed her transformation from a Full Woman type to Ms. Wonder Woman. Her strong will helped her become what she had always wanted to be and helped her obtain what she wanted.

She is a perfect example of the Amazon Type. She views other women as noncompetitive, out of her league. She feels she is just a little bit above the average woman, enough to matter and make a difference. By that she means she is more self-assured than the average woman. This line of thinking is associated with her height and the experiences she has encountered in her life because of her height. It has been a considerable factor. These issues surrounding her height will continue to shape her personality.

Miss Wonder Woman prefers her man to be at least 6 feet 3 inches tall, about 200 pounds, dark-skinned, with a heavy beard and a strong physical body. However, he can't get away with just looking good. He has to be good. He still has to have, and effectively use, his intelligent mind. He has to be self-confident and know how to be dominant without trying to control her. She put it best when she explained it, "I need a man who can tone me down, but knows when to give me space to do what I need to do." A man's physical weight is very important to her. "His penis size is not all that important, but he must weigh enough so that I can feel him when we are making love. And I don't want him to always be trying to prove to me he is a man in bed. He must be open-minded toward sex and have a good ego," she explained. Like other Amazons, Ms. Wonder Woman is usually very private. Women like her tend to live in a hidden land, offshore to nowhere, but they can be easily found by those seeking them. One can find the beach leading to her heart if he seeks to communicate with her mind and not just her body.

Every woman wants this from her man, but as I have repeatedly said, the Amazon demands it. It may be because she has so much more body, height-wise, and that it takes a good man to look inside the person to see the rest. There is a lot there to see and enjoy.

THE KINKY TYPE

THE KINKY TYPE

Kinky doesn't necessarily mean strange. As defined under conventional terms, it simply means an act out of the ordinary. Therefore, a kinky person would be a person who performs or participates in acts that may be considered out of the norm by many people. But a freaky woman is often viewed as one who is wild and enjoys raw sex. However, there is still a very fine line between the two types. According to my survey, about half the people who were interviewed said there was no difference whereas the other half said there was. The only difference they identified was that the kinky woman performed special acts that they preferred to do, and the freaky woman would try anything once with almost anyone.

The Kinky type might cross the line of kinkiness to freakiness, but the freaky type is not likely to cross the line to kinkiness. A kinky woman doesn't usually try different sex acts. She is also a woman who will try practically anything once, but only with a few selected people. The freak isn't as selective. One difference that clearly separates the two is that it isn't always easy to detect the kinky, but the freaky type is the one who exhibits or gives off hints that she wants to be recognized. This is usually accomplished in the way she dresses. The freaky woman will often wear revealing clothing.

For some, there is no clear difference between a kinky person and a real-life freak. What may be considered kinky to one group of people may be considered freaky to another. Therefore, I am going to use kinky to describe the traits of both the Kinky and Freaky type.

Kinky women seldom marry because they can't find a suitable mate who allows them to be themselves. This is especially true if they acknowledge early in life that they are different from most people when it comes to sex. Do they start out in life being kinky? That is a tough question to answer, but I suspect that some of it has to do with the zodiac signs. Now, to my knowledge, there are no scientific facts to support my theory, but I know persons born under Scorpio who are more likely to be kinky than others.

The Kinky is known for her discretion. This discretion is her way of protecting herself from abuse and damaging her outwardly stable reputation. Yes, she is a person whom you would least suspect of being kinky or having kinky tendencies. Publicly, she could be a television newscaster or a behind-the-scenes worker in a busy office environment. She doesn't want you to know what she is, and is quite adept at hiding it. But when she is ready to let go and have some fun, she doesn't hold back.

If a man finds himself in the company of a kinky woman, it is because she has thoroughly screened him about his openness toward sex, or because he presents a challenge to her. Most men in her life share the common knowledge that she is not like the average woman. It is a turn-on for them, but it sometimes leads men to seek her out only to satisfy a deep-rooted lust that no other woman can. That might be fine with her, for it takes several men to actually fulfill most of her sexual desires. She would prefer one man who is sensitive enough to know or find out what she likes or doesn't like.

The Kinky is willing to try anything once, just out of curiosity. She knows what turns her on a little and what turns her on a lot. If she doesn't care for a particular act, she doesn't condemn it. She just doesn't do it anymore or certainly not as often. If a man wanted to try something kinky, he has to carefully explain it to her and ask that she try it with him. Although she may refuse, it won't be because the idea doesn't appeal to her; it may be because of her mood or the person asking. Otherwise, she may save the idea and suggest it to someone else. It is more likely, though, that she won't turn down offers too often, as long as they don't sound harmful. Besides, if a man is bold enough to ask her to try something new, he has already established a good rapport between them.

Unlike a true freaky type, the kinky type is forward about her desires for erotic sex acts. Such erotic preferences could be leather boots and a whip-and-chain routine. Each act has a specific name and is known throughout this close-knit group of people. By assigning labels to the various sex acts, it eliminates the need to describe the actual act. For example, a kinky woman needs only to ask: "Do you like piercing?" or "Let's go around the world." Her partner would know that she means a sex act in which one person bites the other until there is slight bleeding. Likewise, he would understand that "going around the world" includes oral sex.

Most kinky women perceive themselves as an extension of a man's sexual fantasies. A man does not have to prove anything to her except that he is not a selfish person. She can bring out the raw lust for sex in most men whom other women may have found impotent. Because the Kinky has very few inhibitions, a man can live out his sexual fantasies without shame or guilt. While other women are casting aside their men for lack of sexual fulfillment, the Kinky is faced with a supply of men that she can pick and chose from. Most of the time, though, she only keeps a few select men as friends, lovers, or both. He doesn't have to be a good friend to be a good lover, but she tries to forge a relationship based on a good friendship first. She might have married lovers who seek her out, primarily because their wives just don't "do those kinds of things."

If I had to describe the perfect sex machine, it would be the shark. Sex machine, a shark, please. The shark is feared by those who don't understand it, respected by those who have sought them out for study, and admired by those who are awed at the survival of this species over thousands of years without any evolutionary changes. I take liberties here, I know, but in similar ways, the Kinky is feared by women who are prudish about sex, respected by some who wish they had the nerve to do some of the things she does, and certainly awed by the men in their lives who have sought her out for study and fun.

Every woman is capable of fulfilling her mate's sexual fantasies, but for one reason or another many do not succeed. These women are usually too concerned about what kind of image they may render by doing certain things in seducing their husbands. Then too, some men don't want the woman they are going to marry to be kinky. This is probably because they are insecure about keeping up with her or unsure that they can hold her interest sexually. These men usually make poor husbands anyway. They want their spouse to be the model wife and mother, but not to be kinky. Although they may say they want her to be more open in the bedroom, if she does, their emotions soon turn to jealousy and possessiveness.

The point to be made is that most women have some kinkiness in them, but because of inhibitions, reputations, shame, or just being uncomfortable expressing that they like a certain kind of sex, their desires remain fantasies. This is not to say that the only function of the Kinky type is to have sex, but when she does indulge in sex, it is a world of fantasy that other women have difficulty bringing to life.

Caprice is the name chosen for this interviewee who not only fits the description of Kinky, but proudly admits it. The dictionary meaning of Caprice is fantastic notion, freakishness, a nonconformist. It is also the name of fancy car. It is the perfect name for this character type.

Caprice, at the time of this interview, was over age 30, still single, but maintaining hopes of finding Mr. Right someday. Unless Miss Caprice wanted someone to know, no one would ever suspect just how kinky she is. Is Caprice kinky because she was born under the Scorpio sign, Caprice said, "most assuredly." This is true to the Scorpio zodiac sign. It has often been said that if there were 8 days and 8 nights, the Scorpio person could make love all of those days and nights. That may be stretching it a bit, but they could probably exceed the average person's stamina.

"Probably as an oddity," is what Miss Caprice said in response to how other women may view her. "Sexually, I am a nonconformist," she said. "Some women find the relationships I have with men are odd." All in all, she finds that "most women have their heads on pretty well, but some have negative attitudes about men." Occasionally, Caprice may find other women as competition for a man's attention. She views herself as a person who changes from day to day or even from one minute to the next.

At 5 feet 5 inches tall, she would like to be four inches taller, with shorter hair, a slightly smaller behind, and green eyes. In her opinion, her proudest features are her eyes and both set of lips. "Well in comparison to girly magazines and porno movies, I happen to think I have an attractive pussy. More attractive than what I have seen," is how Miss Caprice explained the other set of lips.

To Caprice, a man is only a bore if he lets his ego get in the way of his freedom to express his sexual feelings. She claims she is not hard to please, because she is responsive, knows what she wants, and knows how to get it. As she articulates it, "I usually manage to have a pretty good time." She concluded by saying, "My lack of inhibitions make it easy for me to be satisfied." She feels another woman may have been with the same man and may think that he is a bore. "It depends on where her head is sexually also," as she explained why some women tend to get bored with their sexual mate.

When I asked her if she ever fantasized about being intimate with two men at the same time, she softly yet firmly said, "Of course. What woman hasn't? " After that question, I asked her if she could describe what she saw happening in that fantasy. She let out a pleasing sigh and remarked, "Aaahhh . . . basically, what happens when you have two men, every part of your body is being attended to constantly." She went on to say that at times during her fantasy, she was an aggressive person and other times she was very passive, letting the two men do whatever they wanted. Carrying out this fantasy also created new ones for Caprice, she said. To use her words, "It is a very heady fantasy and then you realize it's a very heady experience. Sucking one man's dick while one man is sucking your pussy, it's --- again, it's a heady kind of experience. All of your senses are completely engulfed in this whole process. Ah . . . having one man fuck you while you are sucking another guy's dick or having one guy fuck you in the pussy and the other fuck you in the ass. Again, it is so total. And if you are receptive to it, you get swept away."

As you can see, Caprice isn't at all inhibited about sharing her thoughts or experiences. She probably could write her own book, entitled *1001 Ways to Bring Out The Best In Your Love Affair.* One of the ways she likes to please is to perform oral sex. She says she does it because she enjoys the response she gets in return, and because it gives her a sense of power. The man becomes will-less when she does this. She dislikes oral sex, however, when the man "just lays there like he is doing me a favor." Caprice ended this discussion by saying, "I like to know if they feel it, because it really turns me on. Some of them taste good too." She enjoys oral sex performed on her as well, acknowledging that "it can be exciting if it has longevity." One of Caprice's other fantasies is being an actual sexual slave where she would have no free will and be subjected to her man's pleasures.

What more could a man ask for from the Kinky? There is a thing called love, she reminds me.

"Real love," Caprice believes, "as opposed to romantic love is a friendship. It comes out of mutual respect, trust, and truly liking a person." All a man has to do to sexually please her is be sensitive to her needs and desires, understanding that there are other things that can turn her on. She likes the back of her neck kissed and likes to be caressed any place on her body. If a man wants to seduce the Kinky, he will have to listen to what she tells him and follow through. For example, Caprice likes to be spanked occasionally, and the man has to be willing to do it.

The Kinky is definitely a lot to handle, but she is capable of being pleased if a man can express his feelings in her company. So if you're a man looking for a sexual slave, search for the Kinky type. But remember, she may not tell you that's she kinky right away. You'll have to discover it for yourself.

THE MATERIALISTIC TYPE

THE MATERIALISTIC TYPE

Remember the old saying, "You can't judge a book by its cover?" Whoever coined this phrase certainly was trying to tell us not to accept what we see on the surface, but to dig deeper to see what was underneath. Because what you see may not always be what you get.

There are similar expressions like this cautioning us against judging a person from outside appearances only. However, there are shelves of books out there that support the contention that what we present on the outside is a true reflection of our inner selves.

So, what do we believe? Can we judge a book by its cover? Not all the time, perhaps, but with the Materialistic woman you can. She has expensive taste in everything, from shoes and clothes, to houses and cars. And she wants the best that money can buy. While it might be difficult to judge others by their outer appearance, it's easy to see what the Materialistic has on her mind. In a way, she has an unsatiable appetite for the material goods of the world. She may know that you can't take it with you, but she knows also that you can enjoy it while you are here. It would be almost impossible for her to make even minor adjustments toward becoming frugal. Thrifty and cheap are not in her vocabulary. She wants to have only the best. She demands only the best.

Most of these women come from poor families. Although they had the most important things in life - - love, family, friends, good health - - they always made a point of acknowledging what they did not have. When they were young, they may not have known that they did not have the best things in life because no one else around them had anything. But once they found out what others had, they knew what they wanted and promised themselves they would have it. After all, they deserved it.

The Materialistic woman's creed is, "I will have the best, regardless." This promise to herself applies even it means she has to purchase the worldly goods herself. Often, buying the things they want themselves is the way they maintain control over their lives. However, some have resolved that they want it at *any* cost, and giving up control is a small price to pay for the material rewards. This is after all, a material world.

This identifies the two basic Materialistic types. One who says, "No thank you I'll get it myself." The other who says, "Thank you very much. Now let me show you what else I want."

The Materialistic woman who chooses to get these finer things for herself will buy or acquire items that either express how she feels or indicates an extension of her personality. She sacrifices a great deal, works hard to earn money, saves, researches, and compares the items she wants to buy.

She is a woman who has an unbalanced demand for her wants and needs. It is more important that she fulfills all of her wants.

Whether her basic living needs are fulfilled or not is another issue. She doesn't necessarily care about the basic living needs. If her wants are taken care of, then she thinks about providing for her basic needs.

The Materialistic can be easily spoiled and in lieu of having someone to spoil her, will spoil herself. Once she has become accustomed to being spoiled, there is virtually no reversing the process, unless unforeseen circumstances, such as loss of a job, interferes.

The personality formation of the Materialistic woman usually takes shape in her early teens but deep-rooted traits can go back further than that. Usually, she was one of many poor youth growing up without the basic needs in life taken care of, and had to do without the basics, like shoes or clothing. Because of this, she vowed that when she reached adulthood she would have everything she wanted.

As a youngster, she probably did not know that most people were poor, according to statistics. For example, that 10% of the world's population controls nearly 80% of the world's wealth. All she knew was how it felt to be without, and that it was a feeling she did not like. So, she made it her life's mission to make certain that she would get ahead whatever the cost.

When she finally reaches the age when she can obtain some of her material dreams, it is interesting to note that she doesn't concentrate on trying to stretch a dollar. Although she has spent most of her life up to this point doing without, cost is no longer her primary concern. She will have what she wants, whatever the cost.

Materialistic's ego, pride, and vanity usually become more obvious and bigger as the number and kinds of high-priced items that she purchases increases. This can, and often does, provide her with a new foundation for her bravado. She can be a braggart, and sometimes vain. She gives the impression of being snobbish and self-centered. She will buy whatever she believes will make her feel beautiful or better than the next person. And remember, that it doesn't necessarily mean she buys it with her own earned income. Everything about the Materialistic woman is well developed and well pronounced. Her clothes fit her perfectly. Her hair is done by the finest hair stylists. Even her speech pattern announces that she is a diva. Perhaps a better description might be that she is a very dramatic person all around. Things are done and said with such high intensity, color, flair. She is one who clearly stands out in a crowd. She creates a sensation. When she moves, her aura energizes the air and casts a spell.

She wants to spur the men around her to action, namely to supply what she wants. Therefore, she'll do her best to attract the interest of a man who meets her physical, and more important, her financial requirements.

Although this description may sound a bit cynical or hardhearted, it is not intended to be, because this is only the exterior of the

Materialistic. Unfortunately, however, a man can generally tell when a woman is looking for a sugar daddy. Although the materialistic woman is usually attractive, it isn't enough that a man desire her as a lifelong partner.

Marriage is a part of her "wants package," but it is something she wants primarily for financial security; love and companionship are secondary. If she happens to fall in love with a wealthy man, then that's good. However, if love doesn't happen, so what? After all, what does love have to do with it? The money, she feels, makes up for all other things. Her happiness is predicated on getting what she wants. That is the thing that warms her heart and soothes her soul. She can be selfish in love.

Although the Materialistic woman likes children, she does not necessarily want to have them. She considers raising children as a setback. She's unwilling to sacrifice the comfortable position in life she has worked hard to establish for herself. She does not want to have to worry about providing the best in life for a child if her available resources can only support a comfortable lifestyle for one person, not two. Part of her reasoning stems from her own childhood. She would not think it fair for her child to suffer as she may have suffered. This is a plus for her character. It is a basic parental instinct to want your child to have more than you had when you were growing up. Whereas the average parent may say it is enough that the child has more than the parent had as a child, the Materialistic parent would say, "My child must have everything and the best at that."

As with most women, there is another side to the Materialistic that people very rarely get to see. She can fool people because she is skilled at knowing how to hide her emotions. Her defense mechanism is strong and maintained through the expensive inventory of material things she obtains, such as living in a ritzy neighborhood; being a member in a social club; owning an expensive car, fine jewelry, or furs, etc. These play a major part in making her feel beautiful and, above all, secure.

As she becomes older, she tends to care for fewer people in her life. As people become entrusting and undependable to her, she transfers her affection, attention, or even her love toward getting more worldly items. This is because she has a need to control what happens around her. When she loses control of the people in her life, she turns to material things because there she has ultimate control which cannot be wrestled from her grasp. She may not be able to control people the way she'd like to but she finds security in being able to control and manipulate the things that she can buy or have someone buy for her. This indirectly gives her a semi-control hold on people. Material items have no wandering minds or stubborn wills. They are subordinates that are completely subject to her desires and are there if she demands them. Again, this is her outer appearance and serves to provide a cushion or salve to protect the soft spot within her.

A man interested in such a woman doesn't necessarily have to buy her love and affection. But he must show some tangible and highly visible sign of stability, such as a good source of steady income, and demonstrate at least an average but well-balanced level of intelligence. The Materialistic is not just a "taker." However, a person must first give to her before she'll feel comfortable enough to share herself or her worldly possessions. The point I am stressing here is that it is not enough that a man spends money on her, but money must be a part of the process. He must also share his time.

Usually, a woman becomes materialistic because she is very insecure. Making her feel beautiful, needed, and secure is the key to her heart and undying love. Much of this love can be bought, we know. But she is capable of the heartfelt kind of love, too. However, she is often quite afraid to love.

For this chapter I've chosen Ms. Plenty as my model of the Materialistic woman. Ms. Plenty is an interesting person who readily admits that she is materialistic. She is a young, very attractive woman in her late 20's. She is articulate and well spoken. She clearly expresses her desires for worldly possessions and why she is fascinated with having them.

At an age when most young women were just starting to acquire the things they want, Ms.

Plenty already had things. She was already experienced and knowledgeable, having set out on a mission in her early teens.

Meeting this materialistic woman was purely by accident and getting to know her took a great deal of time. It wasn't because she didn't provide me enough information, but because I wasn't satisfied with what I had seen and the impression I had formed from judging her based on her exterior appearances. I perceived something on the inside that wasn't reflected on the outside. I saw something on the outside that just didn't fit her. I felt there were things she wanted to tell me, but was holding back.

Ms. Plenty would talk about her positive moments, those good things in life that have happened to us because we *made* them happen. You know, those times when we were in control. When we took the bull by the horns and whipped him into submission, and made our lives as wonderful as they are now without anyone's help. Ms. Plenty readily talks about these instances of overcoming but shied away from discussing things that bothered her. It was from this observation that I persisted in digging for more information. Finally, she opened up and trusted me enough to tell me more about her inner emotions.

She has often admitted that she loves her designer clothes, her furs, and driving her sky-blue Cadillac Seville. These possessions were acquired in her early 20's. To obtain them, she had to work two jobs most of the time. "I had to give up a lot of other things in my life to have them," she explained.

Ms. Plenty is a romantic person who is constantly looking for some new way to experience pleasure. An outspoken person herself, she appreciates any man who can hold his own in a discussion and who is a good conversationalist.

Ms. Plenty says that although she likes to be in control all the time, at the same time she wants a man to feel he has some control. Whether he gets to use it or not is another subject. She prefers the masculine "he-man" type. She feels safe, comfortable, and secure with a man who is not only physically well built, but also a leader. Ms. Plenty wants him to be gentle with her, in spite of his physical makeup.

She describes this as a "hot and cold contrast." And she likes the two extremes. For instance, she likes a romantic man who can also be aggressive. She likes for him to actively resist her at the same time. This resistance creates a challenging environment in which there is an equal force of energy being expended.

Ms. Plenty likes a lot of attention and says she knows how to use power like her father did. She explained that her father was the man of the household. He was the breadwinner, and her mother was the traditional homemaker.

Ms. Plenty admitted that she would like to find love but she is afraid to let herself go for fear of being hurt. She is a romantic person who hides her feelings very well. Although she has never had her heart broken, she said she has had it fractured. She took some glue (money) and patched it up (went shopping) and now it is much better.

Living in a material world doesn't have to be all bad. The materialistic woman has found a way to acquire things, enjoy life, and seek fulfillment. It may seem an extreme way to live, but to other materialistic types, it is the only way to live. The challenge is for the rest of us to find our true selves and go after what we want with zest and vigor as the materialistic woman has. What's wrong with that? Don't we all want to have something to show for our work and our life's struggles? If not, then why go through it?

THE MOTHERLY TYPE

THE MOTHERLY TYPE

There are three distinct types of mothers: the Earth, the Parental, and the Seductive mother models. "A mother is a mother," you might say. A closer examination, however, will clearly pinpoint their unique differences.

Motherhood is being a mother. Today, and for many years to come, this will mean a female parent. The word "mother" once meant that a woman loved, cared for, and protected her child or children above anyone else. Although there are all types of mothers, according to most of the people I surveyed, there is only one type considered motherly.

While I was writing this chapter in February 1991, I was listening to my favorite jazz radio station. It was late, but I decided to call the station and ask the radio personality what words came to his mind that best described the motherly type. He said, "When I think of motherly, I think of the word endearing. I think of someone who is a warm comfort zone." He then asked me if I have heard the expression, "You can't go home again." Of course, I said yes. He then replied, "That is not true. She is always your mother. She has that unconditional love, and when I think of her, the word caring comes to my mind." This type of mother matches the ideal description of many people. Thus, I termed this mother type the Earth Mother.

The Earth Mother is a scholar and lover of nature. Her learned lessons in life come from many years of experience. Her advice stems from the many episodes in her personal wealth of knowledge. Unlike the parental or the seductive type mother, the Earth Mother is not just a mother because she gave birth to a child.

Home sweet home. A hot meal, fresh clean clothes, and a warm smile are gifts of love that an Earth Mother can give, even as a working parent. Many don't exist like her anymore. The female parents of the 1990's are busy being independent, parental, and assertive. The lifestyles of this era have forced many women to compete with men in business and other activities. Some of them can't or don't even provide good parental care and some have even given up their children for adoption. The Earth Mother is not just motherly to her own children, but to neighborhood children. She is the woman everyone respects. The Earth Mother loves people, but her favorites are children. She is a mother to those who need one. The Earth Mother isn't ashamed of her role in life and values it above any career. To her, being a mother is a woman's first priority. Some may even say she is an old-fashioned role model of yesterday. Those same people would probably say she is also someone they wished they had as a child.

The Earth Mother is capable of fulfilling many roles. Sometimes she may need to mix a batch of special herbs to lower the temperature of a nasty flu, give counseling that results in a good decision, be a homemaker for her family, or share her kindness and understanding with a stranger. The attributes of the Earth Mother are not the same requirements for *motherhood.* Any woman can bear a child and be called a mother, just as she can parent a child that she did not give birth to. Not every woman, however, is the motherly type. A motherly woman would sacrifice some of her own ambition for her family's advancement and welfare. The family unit is more important to her and, often, caring for the family is her whole life. It is what she lives for and without it she is not a complete person. Therefore, she ensures her full life by mothering people who show sincerity for her kindness. The motherly type is never outdated. She adjusts with the times and understands human nature. The thing that does not change is her capacity to love people. A mother lives her life through a child. She is always there when we need her, and she never stops loving us no matter what we do. She will chastise us when we deserve it and has a way of making us realize our mistakes. It is hard to fool the motherly type. When we think we have pulled one over on her, she comes back when we least expect it and lets us know she is not fooled. The motherly woman is not just your everyday person. She is not just a parent, nor is she just an ordinary woman. She is a woman who people naturally gravitate toward.

Although the Earth Mother exists, it was difficult to find her in the 1990's. But there were other mothers out there who weren't too hard to find. They are the Parental Mother and the

Seductive Mother. It is important to describe their traits and point out their differences.

The Parental Mother is one who cares primarily for her own family and the seductive one cares primarily for herself. These mothers of modern times are an adaptation of the ERA society. Their roles as full time mother and homemaker have been altered by social, political, economic and ecological demands and pressures. There are some very good mothers like these in the world, but they vastly differ from the Earth Mother.

The Parental Mother is a just that, a parent. She is a mother who cares for her child or children because it is her parental responsibility to do so. She usually limits child-bearing to only two children. My research shows that, sometimes, the second child is unplanned. After the second child, however, the Parental Mother takes careful birth control precautions. The Parental Mother can't wait until her children reach the age of consent so that they can move on. She feels that she has done her job as a parent. When you hear people say, "I can never remember hearing my mother say I love you," it's a good bet that they were referring to a Parental Mother.

What about the Seductive Mother? What kind is she? She is slightly flirtatious and overt in front of her children. She is the type of mother who sometimes walks around her children with very little clothing on. The seductive mother may not be aware of the sexual attraction a male child may have for her. With a daughter, the Seductive Mother competes with her daughter for male attention. In either case, this slightly flirtatious parent can create unhealthy fantasies and ideas for her child.

Let's now introduce our model for this chapter. As you may have guessed, she's the Earth Mother whom I'll call Mother Nature. She is more closely related to the Earth Mother described before. Her charm and wit are as sharp and crisp as an early spring morning. I met this motherly type by accident while on an ocean cruise. It was early evening, and I was leaving the ship to go ashore for the evening. As I was walking, I came upon two women who were trying to negotiate cab fare with a cranky cabdriver. It was a humorous scene watching the three of them bicker back and forth. As I got closer to them, I heard more of their conversation and when I passed them, I yelled, "Good luck ladies!" The two of them looked back at me and both replied, "Thank you ,sir!"

Upon my return to the ship, I noticed that the same two women were ahead of me, walking up the gangplank. We were all late for our return trip back as the ship was scheduled to leave. One of the ladies turned around and spoke to me. "Did you have a nice time?" she asked. I replied that I did and asked her about her evening as well. The lady who spoke to me first, replied immediately, "It was all right." Remembering how I had first encountered them, I asked how they made out with the cabdriver.

"He wanted to charge too much money," the second woman said. "We were not going for that," the first woman added. I decided it was time I introduced myself. They told me their names and we became friendly and cordial during the remainder of the trip. The first lady even allowed me to interview her and she is the model for this Motherly Type.

The rest of that evening was spent in a mini-interview with this Motherly Type. Her friend had excused herself and went to her cabin. The two of us went to the top deck for a midnight meal, though neither of us was particularly hungry. It was a convenient place to sit and talk.

It was not hard to detect her friendly and comforting manner as she chatted easily. While in the buffet line, my brother and sister approached me and asked where I had been. I ignored their nosy curiosity and introduced my new acquaintance. My sister's concern was immediately detected by Ms. Mother Nature, who assured my sister that I looked as if I could take care of myself and that she would look after me. Of course my sister disapproved, but she walked away with a surprised look on her face. Mother Nature noticed the look immediately and commented on it. "Your sister is very protective of you, isn't she?" Her awareness certainly piqued my interest and I wanted to get to know more about this woman I'd just met. During our brief conversation, I gathered enough information that clearly indicated that this woman was the motherly type I'd been looking for since March 1990. However, because it was very late, we agreed to continue our conversation the next day.

Like many women of the 1980's and 1990's, Ms. Mother Nature was a professional woman out of necessity. She told me she would rather be a homemaker than an office worker. "As a mother with two kids and no husband, it is necessary for me to punch the clock. I don't like it but it is something I must do to support my family," she said rather sadly. To her, managing the home, caring for the children, and tending to the husband's needs was the woman's role. There was no shame or doubt in her voice while she discussed this topic. When I asked her what she would do as a full-time homemaker, she gave me the following itinerary:

Go to church and bake pies on Sunday
Make bread on Monday
Sew on Tuesday
Wash clothes on Wednesday
Iron on Thursday
Clean the house on Friday
Have fun with family on Saturday

This was very interesting to me as I felt this was a rigid schedule. Ms. Mother Nature assured me that it was not. She said that each day did not have to consist of the same activities. The point she wanted to make was that each day would be filled with some kind of home management duty. Now, I was impressed.

Cooking, cleaning, sewing, decorating, working in the garden, caring for a husband, and raising children were a way of life that she wanted but could not fully have. Instead, she found herself raising two pre-teen boys, and she had the dual roles of mother and father. I could tell she was saddened by this. Ms. Mother Nature said several times that she would give up her career if she could be a full-time homemaker, mother, and wife. She believed that it was nearly impossible to find a man who would want to take on the responsibilities of a ready-made family. However, she had not lost complete hope.

At times, her mind seemed to wander off. As I watched her in her dreamlike stage, I felt her sadness. It was easy to feel her sincerity. Home was not just indoors behind four walls, it was within her heart. Everywhere she went, she commented, people would regard her as very motherly. All the children in the neighborhood knew her and called her mother. She said a great deal of the kids would come to her whenever they had a problem either at home or school. She would take time for them, as if they were her own kids. The most important people in her life are her children. The men in her life have been important but secondary to her own children. If the men interested in her did not have an interest in her two sons also, the relationship did not last very long. The intriguing thing about the motherly type is that when they mother children, they sometimes mother the men in their lives. Some men like that and come to heavily depend upon that constant nurturing. The problem with that is certain men revert to acting like a child under this influence. Other men regard this as smothering and seek to avoid it. It takes a certain type of man who can appreciate this motherly quality and not be changed by its powerful influence.

The motherly type needs a strong man she can look up to. Otherwise, she will mother him like another child of hers. Miss Mother Nature has admitted that she has not been very successful in finding the right man. She said most of them took advantage of her. They depended on her too much. She wants to depend on someone else sometimes. Therefore, she is still unmarried, divorced. Mother Nature said she would love to be married again someday, but it did not look as if that would happen soon. There hasn't been many men in her life, and the few were not suitable for marriage. Miss Mother Nature said that most men of the 1990's are like little frightened boys. "When I try to help with certain difficulties," she commented, "they feel their manhood being challenged. What I am supposed to do?" I did not have an answer for her. She also told me she is trying to raise her two boys to be men, but she knows at some point in time that they will need a male role model to guide them the rest of the way.

Miss Mother Nature knows that she has a tough job ahead of her. Her biggest concern for her sons is making certain that they appreciate the differences between man and woman. Without a husband, Miss Mother Nature sees her role as mother expanded to surrogate father and sometimes "play sister." It is a balancing act that she feels she must perform well for the sake of her sons.

Her role as a mother is a natural part of being a woman with all of the emotions and desires that go with it. Although she has a great deal of love to give her sons, she needs the kind of love shared between a man and a woman. She believes her sons can detect her longing, and therefore, they try to comfort her in a loving way. Then too, they are very protective of her whenever she meets a man. At the time of my interview, she felt neither son was old enough to be told about sex. Nonetheless, she said that she does not tell her sons fairy tales about life. She believes in telling them the truth, using examples easily understood in everyday life. She would encourage them to ask questions, but she steers them toward finding answers for themselves.

"I don't want to tell them everything," she said, "I want them to think for themselves. I want them to be men and not apron-string children."

Respect is an important issue for Miss Mother Nature. She emphasized that her conduct around her sons was modeled with respect for them and herself. "I would never have a man spend the night while my sons are present," she said. She would not let her sons see her giving a man an intimate kiss. She hopes this example will help her sons to have self-respect and exercise respect for others, especially women. If she had a daughter, she would want the same thing for her. The emphasis, though, would be for her daughter to have a higher regard for self-respect. She said she would not want her daughter to be like her but she would teach her the skills of a homemaker.

Miss Mother Nature is a proud woman and does not wish to think of herself as unique. For her, to be a homemaker and a mother is a great honor. She admits though, this is not something that every woman can do. Mother Nature believes in the old-fashioned expression, "One who rocks the cradle, rules the world." She has a bit of nature that needs tending to. Although it is known that it is better to give then to receive, Miss Mother Nature wants to receive a little in return. She told me several times during our interview that children generally give back what is given. However, it is not just the attention from a child that she seeks attention from. Without a husband to be homemaker for or a wife to, her life is only half fulfilled. "I miss being married," she said. "However, I am not going to get married just to say that I am."

Being the Motherly type does not mean she has no feelings about her sexuality. Mother Nature enjoys womanhood very much. Being a woman is part of being her natural self. For the most part, her sensuality is only seen and shared in the privacy and company of her chosen mate.

THE PRIMA DONNA TYPE

THE PRIMA DONNA TYPE

"Beauty is in the eye of the beholder." To many people, this means a person has an inner beauty that their physical attributes don't convey. On another dimension, the comments might refer to a person's physical appearance, as when a man sees a beautiful woman. He reacts openly and in a certain way, sometimes like an animal in heat.

Men have been chasing after beautiful women since Adam and Eve. Was it her beauty that induced him to be persuaded by Eve to eat the forbidden fruit? Why didn't he just say no? No one forced him so why did he do it?

Let's take today's man and woman, place them in a garden-like paradise, and tell them they can have anything within the garden, except they can't be intimate with each other. Let this be their forbidden fruit. As long as they obey this law, they will have happiness and peace forever. For that law to work, we would have to alter the beauty of a woman's body and eliminate the woman's sexual desire for a man. Why? What do you think would happen if that wasn't done?

Sometimes, we see things or people that cause us to feel a certain way, but many times we find it difficult to explain why. Does it have something to do with beauty being in the eye of the beholder? The sense of sight has a lot to do with the way we initially react to another person. The word beautiful is also used to describe inner qualities of a person, thing, or act. It is also used to refer to the person's physical attractiveness. The Prima Donna is not often used to describe an attractive woman, but this term was chosen because people often treat these very attractive women as so. Thus, we have the Prima Donna Type. The dictionary meaning describes it as 1) a principal female singer in an opera or concert organization, and 2) an extremely sensitive, vain, or undisciplined person.

Prima Donna women are accustomed to having their own way, which in turns spoils them. Men consider these gorgeous women "un-touchable" and conclude that the competition for their interest is too fierce.

The Prima Donna effortlessly attracts the attention of everyone everywhere she goes. Most women envy her and most men lust after her. Everything about her physical appearance seems flawless. Her hair is always perfectly coiffed and her clothes are impeccable. Her walk is confident and her posture always proper and erect, even when she bends over. She might have been a typical tom boy before she reached her teens and became interested in the opposite sex. In fact, she was born beautiful-looking. Sometimes, she looks like she was pressed out of a mold or genetically designed with flawless and appealing features. But when you give it a second thought, you have to ask yourself, how do they get to be born that way? Of course, it is the luck of genes from both parents, but it starts way before that. Underlying this is the physical attraction that exists between the man and woman. Usually the man is attracted by her outer physical beauty, whereas the woman is drawn more to the inner qualities that she looks for and believes he possesses.

The Prima Donna is usually very fertile and generally give birth to carbon-copy children, equally attractive. The ones who marry have at least three to four children, and some even have as many as 12 or 13. Some who stay unmarried have the same number of children but by different men. Then there is that subcategory of Prima Donna who have less than 3 kids and have either been married two to three times before, or are separated or divorced. Most Prima Donnas live very sheltered lives, and as soon as they graduate from high school, they usually get married to some possessive high-school love or become pregnant by one. These observations, while not scientific, are based on more than ten years worth of research and personal experiences.

Prima Donna women are usually attractive to men who don't fit the category of handsome. Good-looking maybe, but not handsome based on most women's standards. Many Prima Donnas have problems with the men in their lives. Men try to possess them as a thing of beauty, or display them like they would an expensive piece of art. The Prima Donna is a woman who is plagued by a barrage of flirtatious propositions, and lies from men who wish to boost their egos and satisfy their sexual appetites. This creates a tremendous amount of social pressure on her to behave like an ordinary person. If not careful, she can actually become the sensitive, vain, or undisciplined person many view her as. It can happen to anyone who is lauded by people for their achievements, whether it's acting, winning a beauty contest, or getting a big promotion.

Living down the Prima Donna stereotype can be hard. It is a constant battle for Prima Donnas who just want to be treated like ordinary people. They know they are beautiful. They like being beautiful, and yet they are troubled by it. Their troubles can lead to jealousy, back stabbing, broken hearts, and even an identity crisis.

Everyone wants to be liked, but the Prima Donna needs it. She wants to be liked for who she is, not for what she looks like. It isn't difficult, however, to become vain when you are constantly being told how beautiful or how great you are. This certainly helped me to understand the Prima Donna's plight.

Most beautiful women don't view themselves as Prima Donnas, and that label should not be applied to all of them. It is the general public's perception that has created the label. However, beauty does serve as a point of reference for discussing the women who fit the description of this type.

I have selected a woman who is "gorgeous" and has shared with me her feelings on being beautiful. I'll call her Donna for short. Donna is separated from her husband, with four kids, the oldest a young lady of 19. At the time of this interview, she said she had adopted two other kids. Born under the sign of Sagittarius, Donna is very outspoken about what she feels and wants. She is a young woman of 35, and stands five feet and five inches tall. She is a very attractive woman although still recovering from an auto accident a few years ago. The accident left a few scars over her forehead and some small ones on her left cheek. Her legs were marred from being thrown through the windshield. The injury to her head has caused dull, nagging headaches since the accident five years ago. Donna has had some plastic surgery on her face, but she is still a very attractive woman.

As she was growing up, people always said how pretty she was and after a while, she began to feel uncomfortable. She felt people were exaggerating or "telling lies." Donna's outlook on life was indeed refreshing in that she believed people should be "natural" and not try to be someone they are not. "I believe that people should be satisfied with what God gave them and not try to make themselves over." Her sincerity was obvious during the entire interview; she never once wavered from her honest tone.

When I asked her if men made approaches towards her, she wryly responded,

"I can't stand for a man to give me a line, and believe me brother, I have heard them all. I can usually tell when a guy is a pretty good person or not." Donna said it is a big let down when a man tries to build himself up by feeding her a line. Most of the time, she said, they turn out to be less than adequate from a sexual standpoint. "I have met guys so good-looking and they are so conceited. Here they are, doing a woman's job, getting all cute and everything. I've seen it. I know about it. But I like the inner person. I do." Donna's words may not be typical of all the Prima Donnas, but I've heard others make similar remarks.

Donna still regards herself as a "country girl" from South Carolina even though she has lived in the Washington, DC, metropolitan area since 1986. She still has a lot to learn about herself, her survival, and her sexuality. She believes now that she married at the age of 18 only because she became pregnant by her high school love. "I was taught that was what you were supposed to do," she explained. "I realized a week later I had made a mistake." Donna furthered explained that her husband became possessive and extremely jealous. She then paused and said, "He was the one always running around with other women. I wasn't doing anything. But when he started slapping me around, I knew it was time to leave." Donna told me it was several years into their marriage before he had started doing that. "You know," she said, "he just didn't have any respect for me by letting other women call him at the house."

Donna isn't looking to remarry, for she has come to enjoy her independence and freedom to do as she pleases. Although she enjoys a man's company, she has not found anyone she can trust. She has said since our interview that she has never been in love, she doesn't know what it is, and has never thought about it since her separation. "If sex is it," she remarked, "then I don't need it." Donna hopes to one day find love. She commented, "It has to be more than just sex. Don't get me wrong, I love sex and I love it a lot. I love the way it makes me feel. But a man has to have more going for him than just sex."

Through Donna's southern accent and dialect, I sensed she was a very caring and loving person who wished to share her love and care with someone. When she said she doesn't know what love is, I think she really meant she has never been loved for herself. Her love has always been kept on reserve for the right person to come along in her life. Many women like her suffer the same fate. They go through life, from man to man, feeling love based only on certain biological and emotional needs. The problem isn't having enough available men, it is beating off the men who only want them for their good looks or as a sexual partner. Some of these that one special man to share the rest of her life with.

I found Donna not just delightful to be with but she was also earthy, sincere, sensual. Did I mention that she allowed me to interview her in her nightgown? Probably not, and I hesitate to do so now. But later she apologized for her appearance and told me that since her accident, she dressed that way most of the time since she rarely got out of the house. "I'm sorry," she apologized. "But I could tell you were an okay person, and I just didn't feel like getting dressed." I assured Donna that her intuition was correct. Then I asked her if she thought she might be looked upon as a Teaser. She smiled and cautiously asked me, "Do you think I am?" I smiled in return and confidently said, "Yes!"

Prima Donnas are like any other woman except they are gorgeous women, pleasing to look at. People treat them special, putting them on a pedestal. But they just want to be treated like everyone else and not have to live up to the standards set by admirers. Just the same though, Prima Donnas love being-beautiful looking, love the attention they do get, and want people to just be themselves when they are with them.

Donna wherever you are now, I hope you are enjoying life with that special man. You are certainly capable of giving back more than you receive.

THE PROFESSIONAL TYPE

THE PROFESSIONAL TYPE

If you don't mind catching her between appointments and business meetings, this woman will give a man much of herself. The Professional is very careful about the friends and associates she selects. In fact, she has very few friends but plenty of associates, most of them being professional men. The Professional is usually proficient with her business affairs, unless it comes to keeping appointments on time. Most professional women arrive at appointments anywhere from 30 minutes to 60 minutes late. I'll explain why later.

Both men and women of the same profession respect the professional type, for she is a strong competitor in all that she does. Most of her social activities are usually business combined with pleasure. She is exposed to many men of different nationalities and finds herself sometimes caught in an arena of tempting compromises. Some of these propositions have helped her climb the professional ladder. She can manipulate, make deals, and still earn the respect of the people who try to use her. The Professional knows the difference between using and being misused. She doesn't object to either as long as she can gain something too.

Most of the men the Professional knows are men who hold high positions in government and business. She is very attracted to people with power and those who know how to use it. The Professionals marry men who are rising in their careers or are already at the pinnacle of career success. Rarely do they marry "beneath" them. However, there are many professional women who marry for convenience only. Like a business arrangement, actually. Both parties agree to let the other pursue their respective careers without interference, even if it means living apart from one another for weeks or months at a time. This type of professional woman is married more to her job than to her man.

The Professional usually has a bachelor's degree, but many have masters' degrees and higher. The well-rounded professional is one educated through formal schooling *and* the "school of hard knocks." Certainly, there are a great number of professionals who do not have any degrees. In fact, I had the pleasure of meeting and speaking with many of them. Both share the same "school of hard knocks" stories and are fiercely independent. Whatever their educational background, the Professional has unique traits and must be perceived differently than the nonprofessional.

The Professional is not necessarily an ERA (Equal Rights Amendment) proponent, but she strongly believes in equal pay for equal work. She is a strong person with high standards and goals in life. Although she may find it difficult to do what is traditionally a man's job, she somehow can maintain her femininity to make (encourage) a man treat her like a lady.

Let me state here that there is a difference in traits between the professional and the business woman. The business woman is a bit brittle because of the strain of interacting with other business people from one day to another. Their personalities and the way they interact with other people, especially men, are quite different. The Professional woman is the direct opposite. She handles business interactions with ease.

The major dissimilarity between the two is that the professional type talks a lot, whereas the business woman listens and watches everything a person does. This is the main reason the Professional is usually late for appointments. It was mentioned before that the professional is proficient in most of her business activities, except keeping appointments on time. Now you know why. The professional is an articulate person who doesn't know how to end a conversation. The business woman would not have any qualms about letting people know that their time is up. On the other hand, the professional hates to be abrupt, because she doesn't want to offend anyone. However, she may break one date to keep another that might be more promising to her career.

The face of the professional is something that stands out. It has a confident look. She looks like there is always something deep on her mind. This is usually because there is some project she is working on. Men will interpret her astute appearance as that of a woman who is unapproachable. It may be true, unless these men are in the same profession as she. As a result, men tend to shy away from becoming friendly with her. She seems to unintentionally intimidate men she is attracted to, and her assertiveness comes on very strong at times. This is viewed by some men as a threat or a challenge to their ego. Therefore, most men prefer someone who doesn't run the risk of damaging this ego.

The Professional dresses very conservatively but with high-quality fashion clothes. This woman isn't cheap, but for the right smile a man can win her heart easily.

Financially selfish men very rarely, if at all, ever get to first base with the Professional woman A man must be prepared to spend a few bucks in the initial relationship to gain her interest. Unless of course, he can get to her from the blind side, i.e., while she's not looking. That is simple enough to do. Her busy schedule blinds her from many things.

For the Professional, a better approach is one that is honest and straightforward. This method is so uncomplicated that she will be taken by surprise and enjoy the pleasant change. Simplicity added at the right times during or after an array of intricate events will make her respond favorably. There isn't a lot more about the professional that needs discussing, except that she doesn't have sexual anxieties. If a man catches her at the right moment, she will show him her adventurous side and invite him to help her carry them out.

The woman chosen for this chapter I will call Ms. B. She is a Pisces woman who has never really thought about what a Pisces woman is supposed to be like. At an age of 30 plus, Ms. B. admitted she is getting rid of many past inhibitions. Ms. B. has found her inner strength and developed a sense of resourcefulness since separating from her husband. She talked about how things used to be before her husband started working on the White House press staff. She would play the dutiful role of mother, homemaker, and hostess for his business friends and guests. All of that has changed for her, and her teenage daughter and son. She has found that the one parent family with a single breadwinner works well even if dad isn't around to bring home the bacon anymore.

Like most of the other women character types, Ms. B. admits she can handle most of life's problems without a male mate. She confesses she does not really like the idea but has no other choice. Ms. B. has discovered since her separation that she enjoys her privacy. Her children are near adulthood and soon will be ready to venture out on their own. She looks forward to her time alone because working hours are filled dealing with Capitol Hill people and business tycoons. She enjoys her work and is very good at it, she says. The men in her life, according to her, have been few but all have been men of status and position. Ms. B. says that doctors are dull because they tend to be too conservative. Sometimes though, when she is attracted to someone, she mentions feeling insecure out of fear of being rejected. She pointed out that she is not a big tease like some other women she has met. Although she uses her profession on occasion to meet men, she confesses she turns into a chicken when it comes down to the real thing.

As a woman well over 5' tall, Ms. B, like most women, prefers men at least 6' or taller. Ms. B. likes for a man to have a well-maintained body and to be good in bed. She hinted that brown or hazel eyes were appealing, but also said they weren't most important. One of the other important things for Ms. B. is for a man to be able to express his feelings. He must be someone she can talk to as well. Ms. B. says she doesn't like a selfish man. She was talking about his financial generosity.

Ms. B. told me she needs attention but not a lot. She enjoys her privacy also. She emphasized that a man doesn't have to spend much money on her but he must be able to express and show his feelings. One way she can tell if a man is expressive is through his eyes. She likes to look while she is kissing him to see if some special look is reflected in his face. The other indication of self-expression, she felt, was through a man's hands. She feels the hands can suggest whether a man is artistic.

She claims her only sexual fantasy is sitting on top of a man she cares for and looking into his eyes while making love to him. This position gives her full control, she says, when there are no barriers to pleasure.

Because she is an all-giving person, she prefers a man to be the same.

Ms. B's favorite colors are corals. They suggest warmth and offer a nice contrast against dark brown complexions. She loves laced undergarments because they make her feel pretty and sexy. Ms. B. admits that she can't always tell in a professional situation when she is being admired by someone working with her, but she can usually feel someone's eyes on her when they are not focusing on business. There have been times when she has caught a man staring at her and she had wanted to stare right back at him. Although she has never taken a man out for cocktails, she would like to try it just to "blow him right out of his mind." She proudly admits that she has never done that because all the men she's dated have spoiled her. Just the same, though, she would like the opportunity to reverse the tables.

The Professional keeps a busy schedule and is generally late for most appointments. Getting her attention is not an easy task, but it is not impossible. You just have to catch her at the right moment. After putting in 10 to 12 hours, her defenses are not so strong. However, it doesn't mean she won't be on her toes. After all, she is a pro and can bounce back when necessary.

For the man interested in the professional type, remember that your charm won't do you much good unless you're involved in the same profession she is. Even then, you have to catch her at the right time. She is a busy woman, always seeking new challenges.

THE QUIET TYPE

THE QUIET TYPE

"Silence is golden," is an expression that most of us heard from our parents. "Speak only when spoken to," is another one. What our parents may have meant is very different from when I speak of the Quiet type woman. She is silent by choice, and when she speaks it is not for everyone to hear. Her quietness exists because she is preoccupied with observing other people. While some of us are busy expressing our viewpoints on various subjects, she is making mental notes about how she perceives us. Although she appears quiet on the surface, her mind thunders with all sorts of ideas and plans to get what she wants.

The Quiet woman can participate in activities and not be noticed by others. She prefers it that way because she does not want to draw attention to herself. She does not want anyone to sense her insecurities. However, there is one area that she is not insecure about. She knows what she wants from a sexual partner and does not mind letting a man know when he is not fulfilling her.

The man who takes on this type of woman had better have lots of energy and self-confidence. He must not take her quietness as shyness. She is as quiet as a cat, and yet she can explode with the force of dynamite. The hunger for pleasure will more than satisfy the lusty appetite that a man may have. She can be considered a woman with a white liver. If you are familiar with this term, you know it means that she has an insatiable sex appetite. If a man is not careful, he could hurt himself trying to please her.

If the Quiet sounds like a sex fiend, you are close. She is not an easy woman to please, but she can be satisfied. You just have to be her type of man. I hope you are wondering what type of man that is. Most men would not last long enough during sexual intercourse to even warm her up. The secret to her satisfaction is teasing. That's right, teasing. Never give her all the sex she demands. Taunt and tease her to the point of frenzy. Her inability to get enough will bring about her own satisfaction. But all of this teasing can cause a man to reach a premature climax if he is not in control of himself. He must have a lot of self-control. What I am talking about here is that a man has to have mastered the art of seduction through teasing. It takes a special man to do this because the passion of the Quiet's heavy breathing is enough to weaken any strong-willed man.

There are some similarities between the Kinky and the Quiet. They are both reserved on the outside, but very explosive behind closed doors. The underlining difference is that the Kinky woman is probably easier to please once you know her preferences. The Quiet does not have a particular erotic weakness. She loves sex for its anticipation more so than the final outcome. The longer you can prolong the act, the better she loves it. To her, climax should happen only because it could not be stopped. She wants to reach one but only after she and her partner are at the point of no return.

There is a distinctive characteristic about the Quiet woman I have not mentioned yet. She is a screamer. Boy, can she scream. It takes a certain activity and a special man to bring this about. The activity is sex and the type of man is a confident one. When she decides to have a relationship with such a man, she is not going to hold back on anything she feels for him. To look at her, you would not think she is the type of woman capable of such vocal expression.

Just what does the Quiet woman scream out? The screams are not just your ordinary hysterical ones. Anyone in ear shot of her erotic expressions will be turned on. So you see, when silence is golden, it is also a delight.

The descriptions I've defined might fit that of a nymphomaniac. This is almost a perfect example except that nymphomaniacs need sex constantly and are never satisfied. The Quiet goes through periods of nympholepsy, a frenzy of emotion. It is through sex that she is able to reveal her inner feelings and reach satisfaction.

So far, all I have described here is an oversexed woman. There's more to the Quiet Woman than this, however. She is a woman who wants love in addition to all of the lust, passion, and sexual satisfaction. The key is that she wants all these attributes in one man. But then, women in general want that.

The Quiet has a tremendous amount of energy and spirit. She is a sensible woman who knows that she is insatiable regarding sex. What I mean is that she is aware of these feelings of sexual frenzy, and she is very careful to not give herself away too easily. She is a giving woman who wants to share not only her material blessings, but herself. Her sense of self-preservation keeps her emotions in check. The Quiet Woman would rather be alone than to have a lot of disharmony in her life. She is not a pretentious person and is fully aware of her physical makeup. She is also the type of person who admits her imperfections. The Quiet woman, although not a perfectionist, is very particular about her men and also about most things in her life. Being judgmental of others is not a character trait, but she is very observant so that she can evaluate situations or people clearly. If you want a fair opinion about someone, ask the Quiet Woman. Her sensitivity and caring coupled with her admission of imperfection promotes a sense of fair play. She admits, however, that she is sometimes wrong in her assessments.

The Quiet Woman will make a good friend. She is a good listener and enjoys people who articulate their feelings. However, she is more apt to listen to a man than to a woman. She is capable of making a man feel comfortable just by letting him express his inner feelings. If you start out being friends, she will make extra efforts to ensure that she does not obstruct the friendship. Companionship means a great deal to her. As much as she loves sex, accord and harmony are also high priorities for her and they are things she looks for in a relationship.

Let's call this interviewee Goldie. At the time of her interview in 1987, Goldie, a Virgo, was 28 years old. She had never been married and had one child, age six. She is an attractive woman, with pleasing brown eyes, dark brown hair, and full lips.

Goldie admitted that she tended to be picky. She had turned down two marriage proposals and was contemplating a third one. When I asked her why, she said because she was not ready. She added to that by saying "I still have a lot of play in me." I took this to mean that she was looking for that special man, the good lover with lots of self-confidence.

Goldie, though quiet, is hardly shy if she sees a man she's interested in. She appreciates certain physical attributes. "A solid chest with hair on it makes him so sexy," she said. A nice smile turns her on too, as well as broad shoulders because they make him look good in suits, she said. She also likes a man with nice slim legs and a tight backside.

She thinks other women are intimidated when she approaches a man to dance at a nightclub. Although some women may feel uncomfortable around her, she is not uncomfortable with them. She purposefully keeps most women at a distance, however.

Goldie views herself as too critical of her life and what she should have done with it. "I'm just moving too slowly," she commented.

From my past research with the Quiet type, I needed to ask Goldie if she was a screamer. "When it is good to me, yes. I don't care who hears me then," was her unsurprising response. She admitted that sometimes, she even goes into hysterics. This relates back to the nympholepsy I mentioned before.

To find the perfect man, get married, and live happily ever after is her fantasy. Although she has never made love to a man on the first date, Goldie said she would do so if she had the urge. Like some of the other single women I interviewed, she too feels she can handle life's problems without the help of a male mate. The underlying reasons vary from one woman to another.

Goldie is typical of the Quiet Woman. She is a screamer. She is generous in sharing her material possessions. She likes to observe people, and she is most happy when a man knows how to tease her better than she can tease him.

Goldie avoids situations that cause disharmony and confusion. She turned down two marriage proposals for that reason. Although she is quiet on the outside, she admitted that she is an explosive and sensual woman behind closed doors. She was a comfortable person to be with. A couple of times, she turned the tables in the interview and was soliciting information about me. So, if a man is looking for a good friend, an ardent and vocal lover, then the Quiet Woman is the one for him. But he must make sure that he is a good and attentive lover and a good conversationalist as well.

THE RELIGIOUS TYPE

THE RELIGIOUS TYPE

"Praise the Lord!" It's easy to claim that a person is religious because she makes a statement like this. Or even because she carries a Bible around with her. Being a religionist isn't indicative of being Christian or being holy. Religion is a relating to or a manifesting of faithful devotion to a religious belief. Based upon what I was taught, Christianity is a religion derived from Jesus Christ and considers the Bible as the sacred scripture as professed by Eastern, Roman Catholic, and Protestant bodies. A religionist is someone who believes in a supreme being and follows a set of beliefs that governs his or her life. The religious woman is somewhat of a complex person. She is a woman caught between two worlds: the secular and the religious. It is the oscillating between these two worlds that sometimes causes her to become confused and eventually lost in the broader world around her. This switching back and forth might make her only world become a life of prayer, penance, and saving the souls of others. The religious woman is not just your Sunday churchgoer. She spends much of her time attending church, for sure, but she also participates in activities that might require her to devote as many as five days per week to related activities.

Not all religious women are created equally. By that I mean many of these women use religion as a mask to cover what they are really like. There are some who have found religion as a refuge from the pain of heartbreak. There are very few women who are religious in the way a Catholic Nun is considered religious. The few who come close to that ideal were most likely raised in a religious background. They either become Catholic nuns, Protestant ministers, or healers. (Most of these nun-like women have been married only once; some have come close but something always happens to stop them.) The ones who do wed, do so for companionship more so than for love. However, they usually choose the wrong mate. Perhaps it has something to do with opposites attracting, or maybe it is their compassion for humankind and their desire to help the wicked to be "born again." Either way you perceive it, the religious type woman often ends up with a mate whose views are opposite her own.

It isn't easy describing the Religious woman for each one lives in a different world of reality. Therefore, I am going to discuss three types.

The first Religious type I call the Burnt-Out type because she has tried everything involving sex and has indulged in as many worldly pleasures as possible. She is one who is easily bored, very independent, and doesn't really know what she wants out of life. Therefore, she tries it all, including men. Eventually, she becomes bored with everything and decides to try religion. She seldom marries although she has had plenty of opportunities to do so. She would always find herself becoming bored with men she could not change, even if she thought it was for their own benefit. This constant in-and-out of relationships causes her to become increasingly independent of male companionship. After a while, she comes to the conclusion that men are only good for sex, and even then only when she has the desire.

After having tried everything and every man, she directs herself to find herself. Often, she tries out different religions until she finds one that holds her interest. When she does, it is usually a church made up of women members who have gone through similar experiences. Maybe this holds true to the saying, "Misery loves company." This type of Religious woman has had an unfortunate life with men. They fall deeply in love and fall very hard when the relationship doesn't do well. Their biggest problem is falling in love with a man for the wrong reasons, for example, just to marry early, have kids, and live happily ever after. Cinderella is another type. She is ridden with guilt feelings of sexual morality, and mentally persecutes herself for her actions or thoughts. She finds salvation through religion and the church people who can renew her faith in mankind.

It is through these mechanisms that she is able to cope with the day-to-day tribulations of what life offers from time to time. If this sounds like a fairy tale, it probably is for this Religious woman. Like Cinderella, she is hopeful that a man will some day come and take her way to live happily ever after. This Cinderella Religious type takes love very seriously and the marriage vows literally. Infractions of either love or vows can chip away at her storybook world and force her to find new ways to fortify that world.

Since the Cinderella type is ridden with guilt feelings, she finds salvation through religion and the church people who she believes can renew her faith in mankind. It is through these mechanisms that she is able to cope with the day-to-day troubles of real-life situations. Coping with her sexuality also presents a tremendous challenge, because even though she enjoys the idea of sex, she feels damnation and guilt about it. To purify her spirit, she buries herself within the scriptures and activities that involve church people who fit within her comfort zone.

Because of her tremendous amount of stored-up love, the Cinderella type finds it difficult to just give herself to anybody, so she seeks out a man whom she feels will appreciate her heartfelt love. What sometimes happens, however, is that she denies her sexuality completely, then she breaks down when the first charming man comes along and catches her in a desirous mood. Of course she blames it all on the devil and tries not to let on that she is in a vulnerable position. However, if she likes the man, she feels it is right to be with him since her true goal is to convert him over. She will put him, through several tests before she submits to him. One of her tests is to make him wait weeks or even months before she allows any sexual contact. In the meantime, he dates her but finds relief with other women.

After Cinderella lands the man of her dreams, however, the fairy tale ends. Her discovery that a man needs more than just a good Christian wife results in her having to make a choice between husband and religion.

Because religion provides her with the emotional stability, she normally turns more religious in her search for salvation.

The third Religious type of woman is unique because she is one who grew up in an environment of religious people and church activities. Most often, family members provided the motivation and teachings of a certain religion. This family member is generally the mother, father or grandmother. Church life has been the dominant influence as she matured to adulthood. She knows about sin and how to handle the feelings of guilt for committing one. She is well-disciplined, assertive, a leader in church, and is definitely a Bible toter. This is not to say the other two religious types don't tote a Bible, but it is a telling sign of this Religious type. I am identifying this religious type as the Naturalist.

She is *home grown* and therefore finds religion an easy course by which to chart her life. Her problems are no less than those of the Burnt-Out type. Her coping defenses have been tested through years of practice. She is still a woman with the same basic needs for male companionship, but her first love is for Jesus Christ. Most of her fulfillment in life comes from religion and her interaction with church members.

The Naturalist feels she is chosen to spread the message of God to all of his children. Sometimes, her religious intentions are overpowered by her aggressiveness to do a good job. She is all work and no play, and this can make her overbearing. This dominant side of her personality comes from her ability to convert and transfer her sexual energies to preaching and saving souls. It is second nature for her to do so. The Naturalist is able to go a long time without sex, but sooner or later, finds herself depleted physically and unable to resist her biological need for sexual release. She will pray that the feeling passes or ask God to send a permanent partner to share her life and intimate moments. If the feeling recurs, she will most likely submit to this temptation of the flesh and ask for forgiveness later. She will justify this by saying that God didn't want her to suffer, and he allowed it to happen. This is especially true if the attraction or desire she feels is to a member of her congregation. Of course, this only happens after the Naturalist has gone through many obstacles before she submits to sexual desire.

You can perceive the Naturalist woman as the one who is closest to being nun-like. She is the one whose religious faith is tied to her motivation to help others find salvation. Using religion to stay off loneliness provides emotional stimulation and eases the guilt of being a woman with sexual desires. This in fact might be true among all of the religious types described. How each type deals with these human emotions and anxieties are what distinguishes each of them.

I have selected the Naturalist to represent the religious type of woman for this chapter. For practical purposes, let's call her Eva. Eva is an ordained minister of the Holiness faith. She said she first felt the spirit at age 14. It was at a Holiness church during a Sunday afternoon prayer service. She told me that she enjoyed visiting other people's homes and praying with them. Her mother also practiced Holiness at the age of 14. Eva's father was not a religious person, and she didn't say that much about him.

Eva admitted the Holiness faith was chosen because it was in this religion that she found the Lord. Being a Holiness doesn't prejudice her feelings for other Christians. However, she told me the Holiness faith gave her the kind of salvation she could not get at a Methodist church. "Being saved means a change of heart," she added.

It was a pleasure interviewing Eva. I felt comfortable around her and she honestly answered some tough questions. My first interview with her occurred in 1979. Based on the information that I have collected, she makes a major life change about every six or seven years. The data below shows a definite pattern:

YEAR	AGE	YEARS	STATUS
1943	0		Birth
1957	14		Born Again
1963	20	6	Married
1970	27	7	Divorced
1976	33	6	Ordained
1982	39	6	Ministry

I conducted a follow-up session with Eva seven years later. At the time I wrote this, in 1986, I wondered what would happen in 1988, the next cycle of her life according to her history.

During our conversation, I asked her about being a religious woman. Eva's honesty came through in her genuine answers and I respected her love for the truth. "I am a woman first of all things," she stated. Eva is an attractive woman. Along with her beauty, she has the traits of a religious woman, i.e., oscillating between the secular and religious, at times becoming confused and losing herself in either world, then finding refuge in religion, which gives her strength and salvation.

Eva also has some of the traits of the Burnt-Out and Cinderella types. She is very independent, knows what she wants out of life, loves people, was married at an early age (20), and has had her fairy tale-like world destroyed by a bad marriage. She confided in me that her troubled marriage nearly destroyed her. Her hair was falling out and changing color, and she was having fainting spells and memory loss, all because she was concerned about what her church members would think about her failed marriage. Religion was her "stronghold," she said, and through it she survived the ordeal of her separation and divorce.

A man interested in the Naturalist should be an honest person with a broad mind, possess high self-esteem, be highly aggressive, and yet be understanding and very romantic. It is important that he be a caring and patient sexual partner.

Beyond Eva's religious beliefs is her natural longing to be loved and to consummate that love. She prefers a man with the qualities that I mentioned before, someone whose cleanliness is evident by their hands and how well their shoes are shined. As she put it, "Cleanliness is next to Godliness." Physically, Eva likes an active man with good muscle tone and a pleasant smile. "I can see in a smile his warmth and whether he has pretty teeth," she commented about some of the qualities she looks for in a man. Eva is the Naturalist type because she truly believes in what she is doing. She's not doing it for her own salvation, but to help others find salvation too.

Eva expressed an interest in taking her ministry to the television audience because it would mean that she'd be able to minister to a larger number of people. Good luck, Eva.

THE SEXY TYPE

THE SEXY TYPE

The sexy type of woman is what many women claim to be. I have found this type of woman to be very interesting to write about and definitely to talk with. Every woman is sexy to some degree in her own special and personal way. However, a truly sexy woman is one who exudes sexiness as a natural feature of her personality. It is inherent in her very being. She is sexy to the core. For the purpose of describing the Sexy Type, the emphasis will be to discuss the dual role of being a Woman and a Lady.

A woman can have sexy lips, seductive eyes, shapely legs, or tantalizing everything else, but that doesn't make her sexy. So what is sexy? What are the traits of a truly sexy woman? What is sexy for some people may be a turn-off for others.

My description, based upon many in-depth interviews and extensive hours of personal observations, is that she is a WOMAN who knows when and how to be a LADY. She is a woman first and a lady second. There is a difference you know. Many women said they believe there is a difference between being a woman and being a lady. These same women, however, also believed it is NOT easy for a lady to be a woman. So what? What! What is this perceived difference? Is it really that important? How important is it? And to whom? And why should you even care?

"A lady will not roll down her socks, whereas a woman would," is how one interviewee put it. She explained further that "a lady is very rigid in her behavior. She restricts herself and maintains a certain demeanor at all times. She has control over how she conducts herself at all times. A woman is a woman by being born female." Why do they say it is not easy for a lady to be a woman? I was told by many of the interviewees that a lady was brought up this way from a very early age. It is for this reason that it is difficult for them to freely express themselves. Since a woman has few restrictions on her behavior, it is quiet easy for her to be whatever she desires to be.

The conventional definition of sexy is someone who is sexually provocative or stimulating. When you combine or add this definition with those provided by the interviewees, you have what I believe to be is a true description of the sexy type of woman. After all, it is not always how the dictionary defines something that makes it entirely accurate. It is also the connotation that people give to a word or to an expression that makes it correct. Vernacular language, or street talk, is constantly changing and adding new meanings to old expressions. Colloquial dictionaries have even been developed to help us keep pace with hip-hop languages and new definitions and meanings of words.

It is safe to say that one who can be considered sexy can also be considered to be sensuous. This brings me to an important point that requires explanation. While being sexy is sexually suggestive, being sensuous means one is highly adept at influencing people through their various senses, not just by being visually sexy.

Let me talk just a little more about being sexually suggestive. The sexy type can be easily identified by just about any admiring male onlookers and perhaps even envious females. There is something about her rhythmic walk that may even suggest to you the way she also makes love. Her hips move in a hypnotic swing from a pendulous charm. It can put you under her spell.

The Sexy type dresses according to her body structure, which doesn't have to be the picture-perfect Playboy-type figure. This sexy woman knows exactly which type of clothing accentuates her most appealing aspects. Her style of dress and overall appearance is purposefully arranged to stimulate the imagination and spark some wild and wonderful fantasies. She not only knows what looks good on her body, but she chooses to take good care of herself as well. She treats her body with the utmost respect and expects you to do so also. She eats only nutritious foods; keeps physically fit by doing daily exercises; gets plenty of scheduled, uninterrupted rest; and enjoys as much sex as she desires (which can be very frequent). Of course, her sexual fulfillment depends on how close and comfortable she feels with her mate. She seeks total satisfaction in all aspects of her life.

The sexy woman feels and thinks sexy most of the time. I didn't say sex. I said sexy. There is a difference but I'm sure you know that already. Don't you? Most women have no qualms about making certain that you are aware of the difference. Ask any woman. She'll make it plain for you.

The sexy woman lets you know in other ways. She uses the powers of sexual suggestion, which are stimulated by using her senses to arouse your senses. She makes you acutely aware that all of your senses are truly functioning. In turn, she is very susceptible to being influenced through her senses. She can be swayed by the same methods she uses to sway others. She perfects her methodology and is very appreciative of someone who has equal skill in persuading her.

A Sight to Behold

She is generally successful in attracting someone's interest by appealing to at least three of their five senses. The most obvious one is sight. She makes certain that you will like what you see. This goes back to the way she walks and the care and effort she puts into her physical appearance. But, "This doesn't mean she will be dressed like somebody out of Frederick's of Hollywood," as one interviewee boldly explained to me.

From head to toe, she knows what goes well with her short or tall, large or small, frame. Her hairstyle will be just right. The length will be styled long or short to complement her facial features or her particular fashion style and personality. She doesn't overwhelm her face with artificial coloring or pack it with face powder and foundation. If she uses any makeup, it will look natural and not artificial. The makeup will be lightly applied and very complementary.

Another way you can tell a sexy woman is by the way she greets people. There will be no fake friendliness or stuck-up attitude. Sexy is open and kind to everyone, with the same friendly smile and warm hello. Her manner makes everyone feel special. Most sexy women may have a favorite pet word they use when greeting others. It may be "sweetie," "babe," "darling," "honey," or some other endearment. When she uses those greetings, you know it is meant lovingly. It is not said in a sexist or demeaning way. It is expressed, and hopefully received, in a way that makes you feel a special bond.

Some women think it is sexy to have very long fingernails. Well, actually, to some it is. But Sexy generally has neat and well-manicured nails. They are kept clean, rounded, and dirt-free. If polish is used, the color complements her hands. Because she gestures with her hands a lot when she talks, she takes care to ensure they are beautiful.

While other women are spending a lot of time maintaining their long nails, the Sexy woman is spending time in the company of a male companion. The Sexy likes her man's hands to be well-manicured too, and pleasing to her sight.

The Sexy isn't the only type of woman who knows how to be sexy. It's just that her sexiness or sex appeal comes out fully, naturally, and unconsciously. For other women, it is an obviously conscious effort, and mostly externally expressed. By external, I mean their sexiness is expressed to attract attention and make others focus on them. Whereas with the sexy woman, she can be sexy without even trying. It just happens. It's there. All sexy women seem to have this particular skill in common. Even when they bend down to pick up something from the floor or when they are just doing normal everyday tasks. They get noticed whether they want to be or not. Sexiness exudes from their being.

The women who spend a great deal of money and time on different colors of nail polish, hair dye, and weaves are usually trying too hard to be sexy. And they don't create the aura of sexiness that the sexy woman has naturally. These women's obsession with makeup and creating an illusion or improved appearance indicates they are either bored or dissatisfied with themselves. They try different looks in an effort to change the image and appearance others may have. Some will constantly try all of the latest fashion looks and hairstyles. Often, it doesn't seem to matter to them if the new look is flattering or not. When you ask one of them why they do it, they generally respond, "It was just something to do. I wanted something different."

However, the Sexy may make changes in her style, but it is generally to enhance her maturity or mood. It is never a drastic change or an "out-of-character" look. Although known to keep up with certain fashions and trends, she makes certain they are compatible with her own makeup and style. She knows her style and works to perfect it.

Like Music to My Ears

The second sense to be aroused is hearing. It is not so much the quality or tone of her voice that pleases listeners, but her excellent choice of words. She speaks eloquently. She knows when to be soft, loud, bitter, or sweet, but she also uses the correct words to get the desired results much better than through intonation and articulation alone. The sexy woman can induce romantic thoughts in a person with just the tone of her voice. Much like the female sirens' songs we read bout in Greek mythology that lured many sailors to their deaths as they became enthralled by the songs beckoning them to shore.

Although this mythical story is an extreme example of the power of sensual words, it shows how sexy women can use words to bring men to them. Who can resist a soft, sweet, sensual request from a sexy woman? Not me.

Heaven Scent

Now, the third sense, smell, eventually comes into play. The sexy woman somehow knows which scents, aromas, perfumes, or colognes bring out the lusty beast in a man. Her fragrance is never worn like an old overcoat. Her sensuous scent clings to her like a sheer flowing negligee. She also wants her man's scent to be nice, light, and manly. The senses of sight, hearing and smell have been talked about as the primary concentrations of enticement. That's three out of five, or about 60%. If she commands these three vital senses, she certainly can gain control over the other two, taste and touch.

Let's examine how she may use touch to ignite a man's passion and spark his interest. Touching is an important tool of the sexy woman. She loves to be touched gently and to be handled in a firm and assured way. Touching and caressing her mate is essential in lovemaking. Therefore, it is important for her to have a soft, sensual body, with soothing hands and rounded fingernails. It is often said that you can sense the intensity of her sexiness even the most casual touch. Her hands can communicate a sensual message to every sensitive area on the body. They seem to know which places or erogenous spots to touch, rub, massage or squeeze. Again, this is not just a trait of the sexy woman, but it is a tool that she definitely has and has learned to perfect.

So far, I've only mentioned general characteristics of the sexy type. Each sexy type will vary according to her own individuality. No two types are ever exactly alike. It's just that these are some common consistent behaviors and traits of each sexy type. Of course, varying degrees of sexiness exist in every woman, but the sexy type has more sex appeal than other women.

Now let's focus on a particular sexy example. For this chapter, I have given this interviewee the name of Eve Aphrodite. This seemed to be appropriate, because Eve is the name of the first woman. There is one exception though. This Eve has the powers of the Greek goddess, Aphrodite. She is the first woman that I have met and interviewed who is a sexy lady and a sexy woman. This Greek goddess was known for her exciting sexual desires and the effect she had on men. Many men and women prayed to the goddess Aphrodite to send them love and lovers.

Eve Aphrodite was born under the sign of Cancer and feels she fits its description. "Cancerians are warm and sensitive people," she points out. "They are caring people who get their feelings hurt easily." She told me that many of her male and female friends are Cancers. Eve Aphrodite says her favorite color is white because it signifies purity. From that, I gathered it was indicative of the lady in her. Although she doesn't think of herself as actually being outwardly sexy, she does think she's attractive. She admits using her eye contact to speak for her in a silent but profound way.

Eve Aphrodite finds other women are actually comfortable around her because many have said they want to be like her. She has had unknown men approach her to tell her how good she looks. She says each time that has happened, it was done in a sweet, complimentary fashion, never boisterous or disrespectful. Men have simply noticed her as a very sexy lady and felt compelled to tell her so.

Eve Aphrodite seems to feel she is attractive and says she accepts and appreciates how she looks. "I'm all right," is how she states it.

Eve Aphrodite has been told by several men that they are attracted to her brown eyes, the way she walks, and the way she smiles at them. I must admit her eyes are dreamy and inviting, her lips full and sensual. And that smile. It is both captivating and seductive. It invites you to her yet makes you hesitate for some other form of confirmation that says it is okay to do so. "When you can win favorable comments from both sexes, then you know you are attractive," she acknowledged.

Although she doesn't like it, she feels she can and does solve most of her problems and handles her business well without a male mate. She admits this because she has had to solve nearly all of her problems alone since her divorce several years ago. She has not remarried yet because she realizes her need for a strong, compatible mate.

Eve Aphrodite likes to please her man and only finds a man sexually boring when he fosters inhibitions. In fact, she admits a great deal of her pleasure is derived from rendering pleasing sensations to her lover. The attributes she notices about a man are his eyes, shoulders, chest, thighs, and, of course, as with most women, the rear end.

"I look for focus and clearness within a man's eyes. I like to give the same kind of communication with my eyes. The eyes are the window to a man's soul. The eyes tell if a person is honest. The shoulders represent a kind of security blanket for me. Plus, I like to snuggle up to strong shoulders. A nice chest goes together well with those nice shoulders. Thighs, to me, signify physical strength. I like a man with nice strong thighs. Last, I like him to have a nice, rounded ass... great for grabbing," she says.

Like a lot of women, Eve Aphrodite has fantasized about being intimate with two men at the same time. This is the one time when she would rather be the recipient of all the pleasure. She wants to have all the pleasure that could possibly be obtained from two men whom she likes very much. It is more out of curiosity than anything kinky that makes her think this way. She is the romantic type who will do things like send flowers to a man or even treat him to cocktails or dinner.

Eve Aphrodite is an East Coast woman who stands 5.3 feet and weighs just 120 pounds.

Her hips, eyes, and smile are not her only noticeable features. She's in better shape then a lot of younger women who are half her age. What's her age? I can't tell you that, but many women in their mid-20's would envy her hourglass shape. Maybe all of that exercising and eating well-balanced meals has something to do with it. Eve Aphrodite is indeed a very attractive and sexy woman. She has all of the main traits to qualify her as the perfect sexy type.

It wasn't very easy to find her, for there are not many true sexy types left anymore. The ones who are sexy without really trying. Remember, every woman has her sexy moments at any given point in time. You are what you think you are for the most part. If you think sexy, then you are sexy. You are only the sexy type when you exhibit sexy traits naturally, most of the time.

As mentioned before, Eve Aphrodite is the sexy type because of her demonstrative traits. Unlike most of the other interviewees I have met, she is someone who I had an opportunity to interview and observe only on two or three occasions. Each time I observed her from a distance, I noticed how people reacted to her open friendliness. She spoke to everyone with the same warm voice and smile. Both the men and women she would greet appeared to be delighted to see her and welcomed her with an equally warm hello and genuine smile. The woman part of Eve Aphrodite creates a natural bond with other women. She feels there is a common, tangible bond among women.

"We go through the same kinds of situations with men. And we can generally share how we feel about certain personal things close to our hearts. Such things could be as personal as how we feel during a menstrual cycle," she says.

"I can tell you what other women have said about me. They have said they pattern their behaviors after mine. They have said that they respect me. They think I have a level head and have an abundance of common sense. In fact, many think I am prim and proper. I have not ever noticed many women who are intimidated by me. When I have sensed that in the past, I seek out their comfort zone and make an extra effort to soothe any anxiety they may be experiencing because of my presence. I want them to know that I am me but still one of them, also."

According to Eve Aphrodite, most men view her as motherly. I think this may be because she comes across as a genuinely concerned person. Those same men also view her as being sexy. She admits she doesn't try to be sexy. I really believe men are drawn to her because she is approachable. However, there have been men with a serious interest in Eve Aphrodite who have expressed concerns and some fear of her mystic ways. She believes this is because she unintentionally challenges their manhood or, more accurately, makes them rise to a higher level.

"Men feel they could fall in love with me but may end up being controlled by me. They always think I have another man or other men in my life. They want to feel like they are in control of me and the relationship. Yet they feel comfortable enough to open up and tell me these things," Eve Aphrodite explained.

Eve Aphrodite's ideal man would stand 6' 7" tall, with medium brown complexion and skin tone. She likes men who care about and take care of their bodies. Someone with nice muscles, a firm backside and well-proportioned thighs, good clear eyes, strong shoulders, clean hands, well-groomed hair, and good teeth are her preferences. Strangely, she does not want a man with a penis that is over 2" in circumference. And we always thought women wanted men with huge sexual organs. Of course, I would imagine that she would not want a man with a penis that was under a certain size either. This is the woman part of Eve Aphrodite that speaks. The lady type would not discuss these kinds of things or any related subjects in public with a member of the opposite sex.

The lady part of Eve Aphrodite wants other qualities that complement the man's physical attributes. She prefers a sensitive, patient, and humorous guy. This man must have self-respect, perseverance, and possess a spiritual strength. These inner qualities carry more importance than the physical ones when it comes down to her selecting a companion or mate.

Eve Aphrodite views herself as a good person who is honest and sensitive to another person's feelings. With pride and self-assuredness resonating in her voice, she admitted, "I want to and I can make people feel good because it makes me happy."

"I am a hard worker and I am devoted to keeping my commitments to both myself and to other people. Many times, though, I would neglect any focus on or attention to myself and make sacrifices to meet my commitments to others." Finally, Eve Aphrodite said, "I'm all right."

She certainly seems to accept who she is and the way she is without any regrets or longing for changes.

While others think differently, Eve Aphrodite thinks her face is just O.K. She answered the question "Do you find yourself attractive?" by saying, "I would not change very much." "The one thing that I would like to change, maybe, would be the small facial blemishes or have even smoother hands and feet. Except for the blemishes, I like my face, eyes, and eye brows. I am proud of my full lips and balanced breasts. So many people have told me my eyes sparkle and glitter. Oh, I think I have a nice frame. I appreciate who I am."

The one area that Eve Aphrodite did not mention is her bottom. No matter what she is wearing, one can see the fullness and firmness of her cheeks. Her tapered waist enhances the smooth oval lines of her hips. Her slender waist, combined with those curvy hips, and full and firm buns together serve to orchestrate that mesmerizing swing in her walk.

This next observation is unique and I had to include it in our discussions about Eve Aphrodite. It is based on an answer she gave me when I asked her if there is a difference between being a lady and being a woman, and if so, what is the difference. Most women say there is a difference. I even think there is a difference. But Eve Aphrodite said they should be the same. While she acknowledges that there is a difference, she is saying the differences should be within the same person. For the most part, the differences incorporate two separate and often distinctively different and opposite people. She summed it up well. "Being a lady restricts you from doing certain things. It requires discipline," she explained. "You can't do what everyone else does. In fact, you shouldn't even want to."

Actually, this is a similar response to those given by most of the other interviewees. Most believe that a lady is very rigid and restricts herself on how to conduct herself at all times. Others believe a woman is a woman by being born female.

Every woman wants to be treated like a lady, but a lady wants to be treated as a lady most of the time. Other times she wants to be treated like a woman, with a capital W. From what I understand, there are times when a woman wants a man to treat her like a WOMAN, and even a lady has those same "times." Do I have to spell it out for you, or do you know what I'm talking about?

A 1990's woman might be one that we can describe as assertive, ambitious, independent, and willing to open her own doors. I have heard so many say, "I don't need a man for anything. I have my own money, my own place to live, and my own car. What do I need a man for? Maybe I can use him for sex. But, I really don't even need a man for that. I can please myself better than most of these men out here can anyway."

Now sometimes this can get to the heart of a man and offend his manhood. However, most men know that if that were really true, there wouldn't still be millions of women seeking the perfect mate and enjoying male companionship.

Whereas a lady might find herself depending on a man to complement herself, the sexy type like Eve Aphrodite, understands there is a time and place to be either a lady or the woman, with or without a man. This is not a trait that is exclusive to the sexy type. It is just that this trait is demonstrated on a consistent basis with the sexy type. She enjoys having a man to complement her life.

Let's summarize what's noteworthy about Eve Aphrodite, the lady and the woman. The lady inside her likes to wear soft, satiny-laced panties. However, the woman in her likes to wear them only for a special occasion or for the pleasure of her mate. Her favorite color is white, representing purity and bringing out the best in her complexion. She uses her eyes, hands, and certain body language to seduce a man.

If she is interested in a particular man, she knows just the right way she should touch him to let him know without being too forward. She is a master of the sense of touch. Since every woman has certain "hot spots," it is understandable that Ms. Aphrodite has hers too. Each man must find these "spots" for himself. Believe me, the trial and error adventure of exploring to find them is just as pleasing as once you have found them. Of course, I simply asked because my interest was purely of the academic nature. (Or, so I told myself.) However, I promised not to reveal them.

To sexually please this sexy type, and most sexy types, a man must want to please her first by getting to know her as a person. He should ask her questions about herself and her interests. He must want to spend time with her and from this, a true love relationship can develop. Love to her is an all-encompassing thing. She does not take love lightly. Although acts of loving can be joyous and frivolous with her, she does not have frivolous affairs. It is when you totally enjoy being with someone and when you are comfortable enough to share everything with that someone -- your time, energy, emotions, love -- everything, then you know the love isn't frivolous. Last, but not to complete a final discussion of the sexy type, the sexy type enjoys as much sex as she can handle.

Ms. Aphrodite openly admits that if she had the right partner, she believes should, could, and would have sex everyday if at all possible. WOW! That is definitely sexy. What a treasure for the right man!

Eve Aphrodite, good luck wherever you are. You deserve a man who truly understands your need to be respected as a lady and knows when and how to bring out the woman in you. A tip for the man interested in the sexy type, just be yourself. Don't fake anything. Ever. It is very difficult to fool this type of woman. If you have all the qualities that she is looking for, she will communicate her interest in you with her eyes and you will know it. There will be no doubt in your mind, and the two of you can take it from there.

THE TEASER TYPE

THE TEASER TYPE

Gentlemen ... Watch Out For This One. The Teaser can be confused with the sexy type. The big difference is, the Teaser teases mostly for attention. You can almost compare her with a professional stripper (she's generally built like one), except that the Teaser doesn't need smoke-filled room, a table top, or a stage to perform. The world is her stage and everyone is her audience.

Although she may not publicly strip, what she puts on her body or often doesn't put on her body leaves very little to the imagination. The Teaser is a big flirt. Her overly friendly nature would lead you to think she sleeps with a lot of men. This is not true. She does tend to attract a lot of them and some are undesirable types. Many find her likeable but not to be trusted. Women cling tightly to their men when she is around.

The Teaser has very few problems attracting men. Her problem is usually keeping one. Although men find her very alluring, they also discover their personal insecurities when they are around her. Her openly daring ways will have men competing with each other for her attention. This will most likely be a fierce challenge to their egos. Very few men can take this constant challenge or testing of their egos. They soon find a way out and move on to a woman who makes them feel more comfortable to be around.

The Teaser is seldom involved with a man longer than six months at a time. If a man is at least 6 feet tall, with big legs and thighs, he certainly can gain her interest and can get in line to romance her. Just as the Teaser uses her body to tempt a man, she is also tempted by the he-man type. You don't generally find this type too shy to let a man know what she likes about his physical build. You may even catch her staring at specific parts of his body. It is usually the chest area, the biceps, and the thighs. Be careful men, with the kind of lines you use on her. She has heard them all. She loves to be whistled at, stared at, and doesn't mind being stopped on the street for a little conversation. She might even give you her telephone number to call.

Because Teasers never make good wives, there aren't that many married ones around. This is because they are too busy trying to maintain a youthful, alluring figure and watching men go crazy. The Teaser spends most of her time trying to be "sexy." This is an 18-hour pastime that causes all sorts of social problems. The Teaser is a very sensitive and romantic person. She merely teases to draw attention to herself.

There are two types of teasers. The teaser I have described here so far is one who teases for the fun of it. This type requires a lot of attention from a large number of men. It gives her a wide variety to choose from. She may select several men to meet all of her needs. For example, one man may be chosen to help her with income tax preparation or college courses; an athletic type may be asked to go jogging with her; a night-life person will be summoned to take her dancing, and the list can go on and on. Compared with the number of men she meets, a relative few of them get to go to bed with her. Out of that number, a smaller portion rarely pleases her sexual appetite. Believe it or not, her appetite isn't as strong as her flirting and teasing may imply. She loves the attention it brings her, but she is not necessarily looking to get involved sexually. To do this, you must catch her at the right time of day and month. Even then, don't be surprised if she appears hard to please.

The fun teaser can be frustrating but never like the other teaser type, the bitter teaser. Most teasers start out in their late teens or early twenties, become strongest in their late twenties, and peak out in their early thirties. There may be some middle-aged teasers around, but not that many. By the time they reach their thirties, they are usually well used-up by a lot of men and many bad experiences. This type usually turns religious after a while. Religion is the only thing left for them to try. If it sounds like I'm down on teasers, I am not. This is merely my observation. You can probably think of someone who fits this description. How does she dress and what kind of walk does she have? Does she play the naive role sometimes? One attractive interviewee had this to say, "A teaser is one that implies yes, but doesn't necessarily mean yes. Some of them dress like hookers."

Let's talk about a typical teaser. I'll give her the name Miss T - that sounds appropriate enough. At age 26, Miss T has never been married, has no children but she has had three close encounters with marriage. She stands 5' 6" in her stocking feet but appears much taller in spiked heels. She makes certain that all of her shoes have very high heels. Miss T said it makes her feet look smaller. Her zodiac sign is Taurus, and she openly admits to being stubborn. She isn't concerned about a man's sign and doesn't use it to determine her compatibility with him.

Miss T is only concerned with finding companionship for whatever length of time she can get it, and from whomever she can get it.

She explained that as a child she was considered the "ugly duckling," and most of the attention was given to her older sister. Therefore, she felt neglected and unloved. Miss T has certainly come a long way. She is by no means an "ugly duckling." She is a very attractive woman and she has all the alluring features to get any man. Miss T confessed that at one time she used her body as an edge to get what she wanted from men.

At the time of this writing, she was reaching her late twenties and finding herself slowing down. Marriage is now on her mind but there were no takers. Men seem to walk out of her life without any apparent reason. She has been hurt many times before and has become immune to certain letdowns. When she would ask men what she had done wrong, they would say she was either too nice or would not respond at all. Some just dropped out of sight. She thinks it is because she is too independent for most men. Miss T believes men view her as a sex symbol. However, she claims to view herself as sensitive, caring and sometimes can be very nasty towards people who upset her. Miss T believes she is attractive when she puts on her make up, eye lashes and wig. Her proudest features as described by her as, "I have 36C breasts, a behind big enough to get a good grip on, full thighs, long nails, and men tell me I have a sweet 'twat'." Even with these features she confesses that she feels insecure about her looks. She is also worried as to what kind of thoughts men have about her. She doesn't know for certain if men are intimidated by her or not. If they are, it might be because she feels she is a challenge and she believes that men don't like that in a woman. To her, most men she has been intimate with have not been boring. On the other hand, she didn't say they were exciting. She has lost count of the men in her life. At one time she would have a different man for several consecutive nights in a row.

Miss T has lived out most of her sexual fantasies. Most women probably wonder what it would be like to have two or three men at the same time, while Miss T can say she has experienced it. Miss T said she gets a lot of hate stares from women and feels it is due to their jealousy. She interprets other women's attitude about her as being a "stuck up air about herself." Other women have been intimidated by her, and she feels it is because she has clear goals in her life and seems to always be in good spirits. This makes her uncomfortable at times -- especially when they give her what she calls "the evil eye," which is a face without a smile. Miss T believes women disapprove of her because she works at looking good. On the other hand, she believes men view her as being a sex symbol, calling her such things as "a pair of tits." She admits it is because of the way she may dress sometimes. Women's hate-stares become more obvious when she dresses to show off her "assets." If she could change her physical features, she says, she would like to have bigger legs and longer hair because she thinks men like that more.

Although Miss T may be regarded essentially as a whore, she doesn't see herself that way and admits she can be very harsh if she is pushed. Being accepted is important to her. In spite of the features she is proud of (36C bust, butt, thighs, long nails, and her acclaimed "twat"), she lists her insecurities first as her looks, and second, the way men think of her. She doesn't want men to think of her as only good for the bed and nothing else. She admits she may give that impression by the way she dresses. She says she dresses sexy to gain men's attention.

She wants someone who will love, care, and appreciate the things she does. It is also her wish to find a man that is understanding, caring, loving, and intelligent. If she doesn't find such a man, she can handle most of life's problems without a male mate. Otherwise, she may continue to go from man to man for the attention she can get. Miss T has no qualms about going to bed with a man on the first meeting. It isn't something she does on a regular basis, but it may happen just because of the mood a man may find her in on a particular night. At the time of this interview, there was no widespread problem with AIDS. I suspect that now Miss T has become more discriminating.

The one sure thing about teasers is they generally know their body pretty well. This particular one, Miss T, knows the time when she ovulates. This helps her to keep from having an affair at the wrong time. She prefers her own birth control method over that of the contraceptives. Another teaser mentioned that she uses her vaginal muscles to make a man ejaculate quickly. She exercises that part of her body from time to time to maintain muscular coordination. Every teaser has one or more unique part of her body that she uses mostly to tease men. Overexposure of that part is usually the method, but she pretend to be very naive role as to what she is doing. For example, Miss T will wear see-through outfits with nothing underneath and pretend she is unaware that people, particularly men, can see through them.

Most teasers are intelligent women and use this intelligence in improving their skills as good manipulators. The "fun teaser" will use a man to provide her with a good time. The "negative teaser" will get a man by his wallet and bank book. Miss T is a fun teaser and enjoys different men because each one provides her with the kind of entertainment she can't find in one man. Miss T says if she had a man to call her own, she would spoil him with romance, maintain an alluring figure, and prepare an occasional exotic dinner. She likes trying out new recipes and serving meals to someone she cares for. If a man doesn't show his appreciation for the things she does for him, she discontinues doing them, or just drops him.

The information presented here is enough for you to get some insight into the teaser type. Both the "fun and negative" teasers are types that need a great deal of attention and plenty of love and admiration before they are willing to settle down to just one man or permit their true selves to show through. The one key thing to know about the teaser is they can't take rejection very well. They are used to doing the rejecting, not having it done to them.

Now for a technique for handling the teaser. If a man meets this type and she makes her play on him, he should go along with the game - for a while. When it comes to the hard tease, he must resist it (if he can) by playing the naive role himself. The more she is ignored, the more she may pursue that man. The next thing to do is to convince her that there is a little interest in her in a sexual way but that there is a great deal of curiosity in what she is truly like on the inside. He then should tell her there must be more to her than what is obvious to the eye. Convincing her of this won't be an easy task. Teasers know how to get to you. If you can resist her alluring tactics long enough to probe her mind, you can win her heart.

To sum everything up, the teaser type is an exhibitionist who uses alluring tactics to attract male attention. Attention is a needed factor for her to feel good about herself. She will do almost anything to be accepted by a male admirer. Her flirting ways give the impression of being a very loose woman, which is only half true. She can be very loose when the moment, place, and right amount of teasing is done to her.

The other half of her is sensitive, romantic caring, and at heart, a homemaker. Winning her heart isn't an easy thing but is a real challenge if you don't become easily discouraged. The fun teaser teases mostly for attention whereas the negative type teaser teases to spite men and take them for their money, or whatever else she values.

THE UNIVERSAL CONCEPTS ABOUT ALL FREE-THINKING WOMEN

Let's examine the story about Eve in the Garden of Eden. And for the sake of time, let's pick up the story where Eve convinces Adam to commit the first sin on earth. Although Eve did not hold a lethal weapon to Adam's head, sh induced him to bite that delicious-looking apple. There were no dangerous items in the Garden of Eden. Eve did in fact have at least one very powerful tool of persuasion. It either had to be something about her voice or the shape of her nude body as she stood near Adam with that forbidden fruit in her hand. Do you think that Adam was hungry for an apple or the sight of her full bosom?

The point I wish to make here is that women seem to have always had the power of persuasion. Although women possess thi power, some do not know how to use it and/or control its force. Then there are others that do not recognize or understand what they have. And still others that don't even know they have it.

My belief is that women around th worl have certain characteristics that ar common t one another. It has been my observation and experience, for example, that women want respect, honesty, and understanding from a man. These characteristics seem self-explanatory, but they need to be explained in detail to avoid any misconceptions.

RESPECT

Respect is usually at the top of the list for most women. It could mean many things to different people. But generally, it means they want men to appreciate their individuality, to treat them like a lady, and recognize their talents, not violating their principles. They do not appreciate an overly aggressive and impatient man. Of course, this list can be expanded, but the main idea has been expressed here.

HONESTY

Honesty is the second important thing a woman seeks from a man. This is the ingredient for a long-lasting friendship. It builds the necessary foundation called trust. Without some kind of trust, you can't get from point "A" to point "B" with a woman. For most men, point B is to get a woman into bed. It is still possible to gain a woman's confidence by telling well-practiced lies, but women don't stay fooled for very long. However, it is very difficult to ever gain her faith again. So start off being honest, guys. You won't regret it. You will have a better chance with maintaining a woman's friendship.

UNDERSTANDING

Understanding is not always an easy accomplishment, but it can be achieved if it is looked at from another's point of view. This doesn't mean we need to embrace or condemn what we think or believe to understand. Understanding comes from reaching out to another and asking that person to let you see the hurt, confusion, or pleasure that exist in their lives. Understanding doesn't allow prejudgment or unwanted criticisms. It is an emotional thing that must be felt and displayed. It is usually the last thing - and most difficult - to accomplish. There are levels of understanding that can be reached if the interest is there. Understanding comes from time spent on research, i.e., finding out what a person likes and doesn't like. It is getting to know a person by their hobbies, their family background, lifestyles, dreams and aspirations, their wildest fantasies, and all the other things that make life interesting to them. It is the common denominator of both respect and honesty. If there is just a basic understanding of women, respect and honesty fall into place automatically.

Time and Money

Another concept is my "Time" and "Money" theory. There are two things a man will spend on a woman: Time and Money. The trick is to balance the two so that you spend the right amount of money vs. time. If a man spends a lot of money on a woman, it's because he is very busy making a lot of money and too busy to share some of his time. On the other hand, if a man spends a lot of time with his woman, it's very difficult for him to make the kind of money to maintain a balanced relationship. In any event, he will eventually lose her. There is a bright side to this. Some women, when given a choice, prefer a little more time as opposed to a lot of money. Although some like to have their cake and eat it too! Realistically, however, they want the time. Money is still a factor, but not a dominating one.

We can't leave out what attracts a woman's interest and what they look for in a man. Bear in mind, these are just some very broad items sanctioned by some women. If you examine your own notions, you may find it very true with you. I have found that when a woman is very curious about a man, she is also that much more interested. The more curious she becomes, the more vulnerable she is to that man. The trick is to have a woman become curious without her knowing it is done intentionally. There are several good ways to do this, but the most effective is through one's own body language. From the way you walk, dress, make gestures with your hands to the way you speak with your eyes and talk with your lips, she has either given you points or subtracted some away. Sometimes, though, it is not always what you say but what you don't say. A man should never boast about his lovemaking. In fact, he should never think he is the only person that can please her like he believes he can.

Another way to get her curiosity peaked is to encourage her to talk about herself. Ask questions. When you feel the time is right, ask one or two of a more personal nature. This has to be done boldly and in a serious inquisitive fashion. If she objects, just apologize by saying,

"Oh, I'm sorry. Did that offend you?" Generally they will say, "No!", but tell you it is personal. You can always respond by saying, "You are right. It isn't any of my business. I merely asked because I was curious about your response. For some reason, I didn't expect you to answer. Perhaps it is best this way. You won't have to worry about me telling someone else." Commonly, they will say it isn't that they don't trust you. It's because they don't know you that well. This can then open other areas of communication.

What about the things she looks for in a man? Most women won't respond by telling what they look for, but they'll tell you what they don't want to see. Among some of the common dislikes women have expressed are that they don't like a man with a big gut, or a big fat man. Most women don't prefer men shorter than they are, especially when they put on their heels. They don't want a man they have to look down on. This spoils their chances to wear fashionable footwear. When asked what specific overall physical attributes they look for, the answer was always: someone at least the same height as they were in high heels; someone who looked good in their clothes; someone who had nice hands and clean fingernails; and someone who was neat and clean all over. For the most part, it was generally indicated that a man didn't have to be handsome, but yet not one that didn't complement their own looks.

Let me backtrack a little. Most interviewees didn't respond to this question as it was asked. They would describe the personality traits as opposed to the specific physical attributes. I think it was because they felt uneasy discussing the physical parts of a man in front of an unfamiliar man - especially about things that excited them. Some said they either like mustaches, or beards, or mustaches and beards. Some said they preferred the clean look all over.

The most important attributes women look for are, respect, honesty, and understanding. You already know about them. The man who can afford to give these three things without fail can win any woman's friendship, and maybe even her heart. The best part about this is you don't have to try to prove yourself in bed. Although no two women are alike, every woman has some of these previously described traits or outlooks about them.

SUMMARY

We are who we think we are. However, most of us appear differently than we are perceived. The reality is, how we perceive something or someone is based upon our five senses i.e. the sense of sight, hearing, smell, touch and taste. The perceptions of ourselves can change from one moment to the next and can be as permanent or fleeting as we want them to be. I plan to help that cause by introducing products and services designed specifically for PERCEPTIONS. This will include cosmetics and health products as well as creations by famous hair and fashion designers. As a registered owner of PERCEPTIONS, you will receive advance information and discounts for the soon to be available products, services and special events. When you fax or mail in your registration card, your registration number will be eligible to win a free PERCEPTIONS make over. Thank you for reading PERCEPTIONS. If you don't see yourself in this printing, wait for PERCEPTIONS II. It tells even more.